SOCIAL ISSUES, JUSTICE AND STATUS BOOK

A UNIVERSITY ASSISTED COMMUNITY SCHOOLS APPROACH TO UNDERSTANDING SOCIAL PROBLEMS AND SOCIAL JUSTICE

SOCIAL ISSUES, JUSTICE AND STATUS BOOK

Additional books and e-books in this series can be found on Nova's website under the Series tab.

SOCIAL ISSUES, JUSTICE AND STATUS BOOK

A UNIVERSITY ASSISTED COMMUNITY SCHOOLS APPROACH TO UNDERSTANDING SOCIAL PROBLEMS AND SOCIAL JUSTICE

ROBERT F. KRONICK

Copyright © 2020 by Nova Science Publishers, Inc.

All rights reserved. No part of this book may be reproduced, stored in a retrieval system or transmitted in any form or by any means: electronic, electrostatic, magnetic, tape, mechanical photocopying, recording or otherwise without the written permission of the Publisher.

We have partnered with Copyright Clearance Center to make it easy for you to obtain permissions to reuse content from this publication. Simply navigate to this publication's page on Nova's website and locate the "Get Permission" button below the title description. This button is linked directly to the title's permission page on copyright.com. Alternatively, you can visit copyright.com and search by title, ISBN, or ISSN.

For further questions about using the service on copyright.com, please contact:
Copyright Clearance Center
Phone: +1-(978) 750-8400   Fax: +1-(978) 750-4470   E-mail: info@copyright.com.

NOTICE TO THE READER

The Publisher has taken reasonable care in the preparation of this book, but makes no expressed or implied warranty of any kind and assumes no responsibility for any errors or omissions. No liability is assumed for incidental or consequential damages in connection with or arising out of information contained in this book. The Publisher shall not be liable for any special, consequential, or exemplary damages resulting, in whole or in part, from the readers' use of, or reliance upon, this material. Any parts of this book based on government reports are so indicated and copyright is claimed for those parts to the extent applicable to compilations of such works.

Independent verification should be sought for any data, advice or recommendations contained in this book. In addition, no responsibility is assumed by the Publisher for any injury and/or damage to persons or property arising from any methods, products, instructions, ideas or otherwise contained in this publication.

This publication is designed to provide accurate and authoritative information with regard to the subject matter covered herein. It is sold with the clear understanding that the Publisher is not engaged in rendering legal or any other professional services. If legal or any other expert assistance is required, the services of a competent person should be sought. FROM A DECLARATION OF PARTICIPANTS JOINTLY ADOPTED BY A COMMITTEE OF THE AMERICAN BAR ASSOCIATION AND A COMMITTEE OF PUBLISHERS.

Additional color graphics may be available in the e-book version of this book.

Library of Congress Cataloging-in-Publication Data

ISBN: 978-1-53616-855-6

Published by Nova Science Publishers, Inc. † New York

CONTENTS

Prologue		vii
Acknowledgments		ix
Introduction: On the Relevancy of Toni Morrison		xi
Chapter 1	Art, Science, and Value: University Assisted Community Schools	1
Chapter 2	On Making *Let Us Now Praise Famous Men*: A Valuable Social Science Tool for Understanding Poor People and Poverty	19
Chapter 3	Community Schools: What Are They? Important Scholar Activists Speak	35
Chapter 4	A Novel Way to Examine Social Science Questions: Casey Cep and Colson Whitehead, Following the Tradition of James Agee and Walker Evans	43
Chapter 5	The Past, Present, and Future of the Goals of Education for All: Some Personal Asides	53
Chapter 6	Historical Antecedents: What Roles for Universities in Community Change	73

Appendix Data	**85**
Epilogue	**117**
References	**119**
Author's Contact Information	**125**
Index	**127**
Related Nova Publications	**135**

PROLOGUE

Education done in and with the community can play a central role in addressing systemic inequities and providing academic and non-academic learning for students, (Kronick 2012).

This sentiment drove the origin and development of the full-service community school now a University Assisted Community School (UACS) at Pond Gap Elementary School, a Title I school in Knoxville, Tennessee. The year was 2010, the date October 4th. Hence 10-4 good buddy. A good sign.

Winn & Behizadeh (2011) recognized "that the lack of opportunities for youth to engage in meaningful academic practices such as reading, writing, and speaking feeds the school to prison pipeline" (p. 149). The school to prison pipeline, social justice, food, shelter, and clothing are tasks assigned to schools that in times in past were assigned to other agencies. Because of this often confusing and fractured system of services, a community school is an effective, cost efficient, and humanistic system to deliver various human services.

The following goals have guided the UACS work in the past and serve as initial guidelines for community schools:

- Provide a safe haven for students to engage in constructive activities, as an alternative to being home alone or on the streets after school. The UACS programs at Pond Gap and Inskip Elementary Schools are intellectually challenging and socially and emotionally supportive.
- Provide enrichment activities that not only address academic needs, but also meet students' emotional and physical needs. Maslow's (1943) hierarchy of needs strongly influences children's and families' needs for food, shelter, and clothing. Homelessness and health issues are concerns of the UACS programs in Knoxville, Tennessee.
- Become an anchor (Taylor & Luter 2013) institution in the community responding to the needs of parents and community members. Universities are especially well situated to be anchor institutions.

The University school partnership demonstrates innovative ways to meet academic, emotional, and physical needs of students and the community at large, (Lester, Kronick, & Benson 2012 p. 45). If K-12 schools need additional resources, why not tap local universities. This sentiment has been proposed by Ira Harkavy and the Penn Group. Harkavy's voice has been strong in advocating for University-Assisted Community Schools and advocating for universities, not simply colleges of education, to work in K-12 education.

ACKNOWLEDGMENTS

I would like to thank Tricia Worthington for reaching out to me and for getting the ball rolling for what eventually became this book. Nadya Columbus followed up, and I began writing immediately. Having written two books for Nova Science Publishers, I knew this would be a positive experience.

On my side of the ledger, I want to thank my daughter, Julia, her husband, Nik, and their son BB Gunn. What little I know about computers I learned from her. I want to thank the many people I met along the way who have been a major part of this and the two prior books published by Nova Science Publishers. I want to acknowledge my son, Will, who lives and works in Juneau, Alaska. I want to thank him for what he has taught me as an Indian culturalist in Juneau.

Kathi Pauling for her adherence to very high standards for my writing and for everything she does. I thank you readers and hope you will read this book and in some small way will be inspired to become a scholar activist. Finally, to Nicole Matis who typed from my script I say thank you because without your diligent work always with a smile and laugh, this book would not have seen the light of day.

Thanks to you one and all those named and those not.

I am writing this after two invasive surgeries. Writing has become a flow experience for me, even though writing is not a risk taking, athletic behavior, it does have an exhilarating association with it. Csikszentmihalyi (1970) described flow as an optimal experience. For me, a flow experience has been hitting a flat backhand in tennis just like Roger Federer. The flow experience requires intense concentration and may become addictive. Think of positive addictions as tennis, running, and possibly even writing books, articles, and essays. I hope you the reader enjoy this book as much as I have writing it, a true flow experience.

RFK
Knoxville, TN
December, 2019

INTRODUCTION:

ON THE RELEVANCY OF TONI MORRISON

IN HONOR AND MEMORIAM OF TONI MORRISON

The great American novelist and Nobel Laureate used breathtaking prose and a clear moral vision in pursuit of a more human and just world (T. Jones 2019).

All of her novels center on the lives of people who struggle to find their place in a country that doesn't always afford them true ownership on the land upon which they find themselves rooted. They are treated like unwelcome but necessary tenants that America requires to function (Jones 2019 p. 44).

May those works set the readers of this book to learn and have a theory to bring about transformative social change, bring in the marginalized and outsiders, and make for equality and justice for all. Our country does not need any further reminders that the time for positive social change is beyond now.

Chapter 1

ART, SCIENCE, AND VALUE: UNIVERSITY ASSISTED COMMUNITY SCHOOLS

Only by happenstance did I stumble on to an article by Malcolm Gladwell entitled "The Crooked Ladder: The Criminals Guide to Upward Mobility" (2014). Gladwell unites scholars whose theoretical models are quite far apart, including Erving Goffman, father of Alice Goffman, and Robert Merton, a structural functionalist at Columbia University. In 1957 Merton developed a paradigm of means and goals that focused on systemic and cultural barriers to successful life. Richard Cloward and Lloyd Ohlin followed Merton's work, and in the 2016 election, conservative pundits Mark Levin and Michael Savage strongly attacked this work as pandering to marginalized folks and offered up their neo-liberal arguments as counter narratives to what Robert Merton proffered in 1957. So what did Merton's paradigm of functional analysis say?

	Means	Goal
Conformity	+	+
Innovation	-	+

Ritualism	+	-
Retreatism	-	-
Rebellion	±	±

Gladwell in his article is most taken by innovation which I discuss last here.

Conformity – The means and the goals of society are accepted; hard work, education, and employment are what social reproduction in schools and socialization by the family are active agents here.

Ritualism – The means prescribed by society are followed but the goals are not. Success comes from inner experiences not societal recognition. Organic farmers, Quakers, and Mennonites might be considered ritualists.

Retreatism – This societal option denies both means and goals. Drug users and career alcoholics are a fit here. People who live off the grid are part of this alternative opportunity.

Rebellion – This cultural choice denies both means and goals but develops new means and new goals. The shakers in Kentucky and the Farm established by Richard Gaskin in middle Tennessee in the 1960s might be examples. In the corrupt political environment, we might see a political movement that is successful that is a Mertonian option that is one of authentic rebellion. Now what did Gladwell see in innovation that dovetails with Alice Goffman's *On the Run*.

Gladwell states, many Americans, particularly those at the bottom of the heap, believed passionately in the promise of the American dream…the kinds of institutions that could reward hard work and promote advancement were closed to them. They found alternative ways of pursuing the American dream, (Gladwell 2014). The connection to Alice Goffman is a complex one. Gladwell in discussing innovation avers that criminal activity was not a rejection of legitimate society. It was an attempt to join in, (Gladwell 2014). Keep in mind that innovation is about the acceptance of goals but through now sanctioned societal means.

Alice Goffman's six-year odyssey on the ground in Philadelphia uncovered a change in policing more so than in criminal behavior, which resulted in the concentrated arrests of young black males in the 1920s. James Forman Jr. (2017) in *Locking Up Our Own*, a Pulitzer Prize winner in 2018, cogently describes Bill Clinton's alliances with the black bourgeoisie resulted in the mass arrests of young black men. Forman Jr., a former public defender in Washington D.C., found that the judge, jury, attorneys, and defendants were all black. These current authors (except for Merton) all have valuable and complex data and theory for scholar activists of today.

AN ECLECTIC LOOK AT SOCIAL SCIENCE: THE CASE OF COMMUNITY SCHOOLS

"I know I am making the choice most dangerous to an artist in valuing life over art."
-    James Agee

With these words James Agee acknowledges the restless journey his biography would encompass. Poet, novelist, journalist, film critic, and social activist. All of these roles shaped Agee's writings and put him in an unorthodox way in what this book refers to as engaged scholar activists.

Good teaching alone cannot mitigate the effects of poverty. Teachers on their own cannot meet the myriad needs that students bring to school. As Blenza Davis, principal at Sarah Moore Greene School in the 1990s, said those kinds don't leave their problems at home.

This vignette is one that shows the complexity of human behavior and that what appears evident in human service work is not.

The fifth grader who started fights at school almost daily was brought to the attention of the University Assisted Community School staff. The precipitating event was that he threatened his teacher, and as she said, if he had a gun he would have killed me. Here is what we learned through active listening:

- The boy was living with his mother, two younger siblings, and the mother's boyfriend. The mother's sister was incarcerated and pregnant. The newborn will live with the family while the mother is incarcerated.
- The eleven-year-old boy was put in charge of the younger siblings. When something went wrong, the man living in the house beat him with a belt buckle.
- Some human service worker not knowing the entire story wrote that the boy needed anger management. This was absolutely in error.
- As the UACS team learned the whole story, interventions were devised and implemented.
- They included a stern warning that if the beatings continued, both adults would be sent to prison for parole violations. We had the parole officer check into the home environment.
- The boy attended the after-school program, and arrangements were made for the younger siblings.
- The boy passed fifth grade and called the teacher he threatened to tell her he was in school. Her comment, "I would adopt him if I could." A success.

"Looking is harder than it looks because looking is not innocent."
- Baldwin Lee

Research and service that is based on social activism [Kronick 2018, (Kronick in press) and social justice Auerbach 2012] is based on

Art, Science, and Value

an underlying precept that if one is looking for problems in living, all they have to do is look. Problems are conceptualized as problems in living as opposed to problem people. This line of thought leads to deficit thinking. Move the system and those who create social policy and do human service work look for deficits in neighborhoods, families, or individuals. This leads to self-fulfilling prophecies where what is being examined appears. The system created what it was searching for. When it is assumed that third grade students can't read because they are lazy and not motivated. When this happens, this system created poor readers. Quite possibly this problem in reading is due to a parent losing a job, a sibling with asthma keeping family members up all night with their coughing. Clearly, what happens in one system may be caused by what happens in other systems. This leads to a systemic view of society and a disavowal of victim blaming (Ryan 1971).

The following are concepts that make for a unified system of policy and interventions. These concepts are considered to be extremely important, so a concise workable description is presented.

- Self-fulfilling prophecy – an example such as if people of color moving into a neighborhood *causes* housing values to drop. What in fact happens is that home owners tend to put their homes up for sale, leading to an increase in supply over demand, leading to a drop in price. The initial correlation was spurious. The cause resided in an increase in supply relative to demand. From third grade reading to housing prices, self-fulfilling prophecies are viable concepts to consider, both theoretically and empirically.
- Problems in living vs. problem people – Problem people are marginalized, stigmatized, and ostracized. When calling people who want to come to this country horrible epithets such as the N-word, anti-Semitic, or LGBTQ+, they are open targets for all types of prejudices and discrimination. The audiences who label

folks have the power to do so by shifting the focus of interventions to the people with problems, not problem people. A notable exception to this line of thinking is deafness. Deaf folks see sign language as superior to spoken speech. From the perspective of the deaf community, deafness is a cultural difference, not a handicap. For a more complete discussion of labelling theory with a full discussion on society at large, significant others, and agents of social control, see Edwin Schur's (1971) *Crimes Without Victims. What Psychotherapists Should Know About Disabilities* is an excellent source on deafness and other disabilities.

- Deficit thinking and victim blaming – Too often, human services and the society that generates them tend to see people with problems in living as having only deficits and not strengths. The culture of poverty which became popular in the 1960s and politicized by senator Daniel Patrick Moynihan saw only deficits in black families. Both black men and women were blamed for the state of the black family. Policies aimed at black families spilled over into the criminal justice system. The overabundance of young black men in prison and boys in special education and correctional schools is a national tragedy today. This concept of the culture of poverty was based on a study done in a small Mexican village. For a complete discussion of the culture of poverty, see Oscar Lewis (1952) and Michelle Alexander's, *The New Jim Crow* (2012).

Systems theory is best exemplified by the voluminous work of Urie Bronfrenbrenner (1979). His work on the ecology of human development where behaviors that occur in one system are caused by behaviors in other systems is important to all. Our community schools have found that challenged children must navigate many systems daily. This systems navigation can replace a focus on personality. This emphasis on systems works so that systems approaches supersede victim blaming.

This book begins with acknowledging the complexity and importance of looking and of being out there away from the confines of the university campus. This book is about uniting social science theory and the arts, including art, photography, music, dance, and glass blowing. The arts have the power to open cracks in social norms and hidden injustice by provoking soulful reflection and reimagination of the world (Eisner 1998). Keep in mind the opening quote from photographer Baldwin Lee where he states looking is not innocent. Eliot Eisner, a pioneer in constructing a social science model, states that imaginative extrapolation involves using what one sees to generate theoretical interpretations that give the particular situation a fresh significance. Imaginative extrapolation provides the material through which new perspectives are made available. Facts are made meaningful, and coherence is made possible (Eisner 1998 p. 153).

Art and the artist provide insights into human behavior. James Agee and Walker Evans in *Let Us Now Praise Famous Men* utilize various forms of literature such as literature reviews, adapting movies, and writing. Agee's populist views along with his anti-establishment style put him at odds with the mainstream values of society. Agee was born in Knoxville, Tennessee, went to private school in the Sequatchie Valley of East Tennessee and New Hampshire, then graduated from Harvard University. He lived a life of fury with wine and women and died in a New York City cab. His volatile personal life played out in his writings. Two instances stand out in idealism that help explain the relationship between writer and what is written. All this is to say how do scholar activist researchers engage with what they are working to learn from and work to bring about social justice. One needs to know oneself.

Agee and Evans take a break from Hale county and go to Birmingham. While driving, they see a girl who Agee conjures up as a whore. He never acts on this situation and leaves it only at the level of an idea. Interestingly enough, Agee does act on his being drawn toward Emma who he finds attractive. She is unhappily married and is treated poorly by her husband. Agee also fantasizes what it would be like to fight with some young boys who he comes across. All of these experiences effect how Agee feels and writes about the folks of Hale county. This same process when writing about challenged children in challenged schools in challenged neighborhoods. Insights into Walker Evans' personal life are more visual than verbal. One exception is Walker Evans asks the Ricketts if they can come and stay with them which they do. It may be that having a camera is a good way to start a conversation. Baldwin Lee, a noted photographer, tells that he saw an arbor and some sleep. He stops and speaks with the tenant on the property. Lee tells him that a photographer cannot pass up an arbor and sheep. During this adventure, Lee notes that the tenant has put tires into the ground so as to prevent erosion. He asks Mr. Fulton if he owns the land. The response is no he doesn't. Why then does he go through all this work for land he does not own. The tenant said God gave me land and so I must take care of it. Upon entering the house, Lee finds that Mrs. Fulton had stacks of cereal boxes stacked in the kitchen. They all had pictures on them, and they kept her company when she ate as her children had all moved away. On first blush this looks irrational. It is very rational.

WHAT IS A COMMUNITY SCHOOL?

Kronick in 2019 has attempted to develop and present a definition. Consensus on this is challenging. A clear and workable definition is tantamount to success for the community school movement. In a meeting at the University of Pennsylvania, there was a spirited discussion on what a community school is. The people at the table were from states as disparate as California, Wisconsin, Pennsylvania, New

Art, Science, and Value

Mexico, Indiana, and Tennessee. This group struggled with but did not come to any type of consensus on this important topic. Definition is definitely a necessary first step in commencing this important journey. Charter schools in some instances have come up with a definition with some consensus on a definition. A comprehensive piece of research (Maier et al. 2017) has come up with a workable definition that may suit those working to begin a community school. The following are characteristics this group came up with.

- a curriculum that is student-centered. Issues such as high stakes testing versus good teaching with involvement between teachers and students are critical issues to be discussed. Closure and enactment of teaching strategies that value and implement the "culture and life experiences of the children into the curriculum."
- Social services are provided at the school. This is efficient and effective where the parents do not miss work and the child is out of class for a short period of time. The school as a hub of services minimizes the fracturing of services and demystifies human service systems for children, families, neighborhoods, and communities.
- Social justice is a central theme, value, and goal of community schools. Providing a level playing field and closing the opportunity gap are both parts of community schools and their drive for social justice. Collaborating with criminal justice, mental health, and welfare services is how community schools make social justice a capstone of their programs.

Juvenile justice can keep children out of state custody through early interventions and helping schools with children who have been truant or unruly. A competent caseworker can help children whose major impediment to school success is living in poverty. Kronick and Hargis

(1998) propose a curriculum that is designed to keep children healthy, out of jail, and employed. This curriculum requires good teaching and coursework that utilizes the assets and liabilities of children's environments.

Teachers would rather see blood than headlice. This vignette is about how the UACS played a leadership and collaborative role in working with two young sisters who were coming to school with headlice. They would be sent to the clinic and then sent home. This little present had the following repercussions. 1. Other students weren't allowed in the clinic. This caused multiple problems for the school nurse. 2. Students knew why the girls were being sent from their class to the clinic. As an aside, the UACS played a major role in the construction of the clinic from a closet. 3. The girls would not be able to do well on state tests. A brief synopsis of what was done is presented. A citation for the original article is given at the end of this vignette.

Keeping the family out of state custody requires collaboration, systems approaches, and family counseling. Collaboration among the professionals who attended a meeting was necessary to help the mother of the two girls. One measure of success was the behavior of the girls and their academic progress. This of course was the presenting problem. The presenting problem is often part of a series of problems. People often have multiple problems. Also, we must remember about assets and not to focus on deficit thinking. Systems thinking is critically important because the problems in today's school systems are so complicated that an individual level of thinking will not work (Kronick 2006 p. 109).

The following was generated by professionals from the school, a probation officer, the UACS, the neighborhood policeman, and the mother. p. 110.

This vignette illustrates the interplay of systems thinking, prevention, and collaboration. This vignette is in the Educational Forum 2006 volume 70 pp. 104-115.

Art, Science, and Value

The issues of this vignette are as true today as they were in 2006.

This vignette is an example of collaboration among agencies and personnel that worked to prevent two young girls who were likely to be suspended from school from doing so. In fact, these two girls passed the state test and went on to the next grade. Mental health issues are a highly salient issue for children and families in challenged schools and who live in challenged neighborhoods. Mental illnesses locked into hardcore poverty issues are wicked problems that our society must control. The community school is an excellent lynchpin for this odious and necessary challenge. Programming for these noncurricular issues when working with school educators from kindergarten to high school can surely make for academic success and healthy living.

- Parent and community involvement are always asked about in public forums about the successes of community schools. The answer after twenty years of doing this work—when it comes to evening programs such as theater and music performances and science experiments, they do come. On other situations, parent involvement sometimes is not what is hoped for. Jobs, anxiety, and even fear account for parents not coming to participate in school events. We have learned that Latinx men are more likely to come to the school during standard time as opposed to daylight time for one simple reason—they are working. One of the best opportunities to learn family interaction is when families pick up their children at school. Observations at these events is an excellent learning experience that has to do with stereotypes that surround these circumstances. There is no question that there is love in those families. Being out there allows for accurate understanding of what is as opposed to erroneous stereotypes.
- A community school is a seamless organization where what we call shift one (school principal) and shift two (after school

coordinator) work collaboratively and see the children as our children. My experience early on was when something went awry, the principal claimed the community school kiddos must have done it. Through diligent work by shift one and shift two staff, this hasn't happened for several years.

A FEW QUICK DITTIES

Good schools are good for the community. The community with the best schools wins.

One of the toughest audiences I have spoken to is the League of Women Voters, made up mostly of older women. Their most penetrating question at that time was why should we be concerned with K-12 education, our children have graduated. In our community, 25% of families have children in school. I sense this is near the national average. My response to them was who among you eats in restaurants? After a unanimous raising of hands, I asked how many want the food preparer to be able to read the sign in the bathroom saying employees must wash their hands? Needless to say, this response got the desired response for why we want to have an educated community at the most basic level. Enough said…

School failure is a systems failure and requires a broader, bolder approach to improving school performance…any attempt at improving schooling must address the interlocking and overlapping systems that create the underperforming conditions (Noguera 2011).

Hence, social clubs, non-profit organizations, and universities have a role in K-12 education and transforming conditions that merely maintain the status quo. We know what needs to be done. It's now time to have the wherewithal to do it and get it done. The "get it done" is not charters and vouchers but rather schools that are public schools with top-down, bottom-up, and lateral communication.

Art, Science, and Value   13

How does the university interface with K-12 students?

- Get university resources, including faculty research and general expertise involved in schools. Nutrition, public health, psychology, sociology, medicine, recreation, nursing, and many others can do this work.
- Get involved in the politics of education. What are the politics of charters, vouchers, community schools? The education of poor children is a political morass. Cities like Memphis and New Orleans have subscribed on a large scale to charter schools. There is no doubt that nefarious parties are making a great deal of money from this situation.
- Just as faculty can get involved in research with schools, they can get involved with communities doing the same. Working with communities requires effort as most faculty are more comfortable working on campus than in the community or with schools. Communities want problems solved while universities work to increase knowledge in their respective fields.

Keep in mind that psychology was in schools until soldiers returned from World War II. Psychology never returned as they worked with veterans who needed their help after seeing combat. Monies were also directed to those soldiers and their needs.

The urban crisis has created an imperative for urban universities, especially those in poor communities, to take the lead in revitalizing central cities (Wofford 1970). Taylor & Luter (2013) aver that civic engagement and service learning do not solve the problems facing blacks and other oppressed minorities. Taylor & Luter may well push for a paradigm shift from a poverty model to a civil rights model becoming the transformative model for civic engagement and service learning by the university.

14   *Robert F. Kronick*

James Comer, a psychiatrist at Yale University and a colleague of Edward Zigler, founder and developer of Head Start, has the following to say regarding school-university interaction:

- The school is the most natural place to help children for there is no stigma attached (1). Kronick (2005) adumbrated that if parents/guardians had a history of good experiences at the school, they would return in the future. One of our principals (S.E.) shared that with the arrival of the UACS program, she got very few complaints from parents.
- Schools are more accessible to systemic change than the family (2). Kronick & Basma (2018) discuss the importance of working with both systems as much as economic, religious, and political systems. Bronfrenbrenner (1979) is a superb source here. Kronick & Basma (2018) illustrate how they entered these systems. The community school brought in nontraditional people during nontraditional hours. At this time, schools began to realize they could not do what was needed by themselves.
- Difficult school interactions between students and schools compound cognitive skill and knowledge in development and lead to early school failure. Comer (1996) and Bronfrenbrenner (1979) are on the same side on this one. Charles Hargis strongly supported the curriculum as the source of contention here. He claimed that a lock step curriculum where students all matriculate the same curriculum guaranteed that some students would fail. He stated the curriculum should be tailored to the child (Kronick & Hargis 1998).

ENGAGED SCHOLARSHIP AND COMMUNITY SCHOOLS KRONICK (2018 & 2020)

Books on engaged scholarship service learning and community schools adumbrate the need for universities, especially research one universities to leave their pristine homes on the hill and become involved in the needs of their communities. The solving of social problems was to be the most important task of these universities. These universities were to be anchor institutions. Institutions who made commitments to their local communities and did not move (Taylor & Luter 2013). Universities and hospitals are examples of anchor institutions. These universities became civically engaged and their ethos was to work for social justice through community engagement (Kronick 2018, 2020) and service learning (Kronick, Cunningham, & Gourley 2011): (Kronick & Cunningham 2017). Urban Regime Theory (2008) avers that a few college professors do the work of the university in the community rather than the university doing the civically engaged work along with service learning. By being out there, engaged scholars learn about the culture of people who are different from themselves. *Appalachian Reckoning* is a book where the authors are working to correct the image of hillbillies created by J. D. Vance. As one contributor said, an elegy is an ode to the dead.

Community engagement according to the Center for Disease Control and Prevention is the process of working collaboratively with and through community groups to address issues affecting well-being (CDC 1994). Following this line of thought, Harkavy & Donovan (2005) assert that the time has come to discuss where American higher education is going. Individuals in academia can no longer afford to be removed from the crises within their communities. Faculty, staff, and students should be involved in the betterment of their community broadly defined.

Agee, Vance, and Appalachian Reckoning

These three on their face appear incongruous, but a key theme of this book is that these odd couples open the doors to transformative change and a move toward social justice. Engaged universities are a major force in working toward a socially just society. It is an ongoing process with objectives and goals and an end point that is constantly in motion. Agee and Evans began the story of rural Alabama with their eye on an article for Fortune Magazine which was rejected but eventually was published as a book. Agee and Evans came from privileged backgrounds, but early on they became advocates for the poor and the challenged in our society. Their reflections, thoughts, and actions while engaged with famous peoples and communities are stunningly relevant in our current era of working with challenged folks systematically on social problems. Our current focus on community schools, engaged scholars, and scholar activists was borne from similar perspectives of the learner and the people who have been selected for study. Joy Dryfoos had a similar role to Agee and Evans in their zeal to tell the stories of poor rural whites in Alabama in 1936 or challenged children and families from the 1950s to the current moment. Dryfoos saw the school as a hub of services where the focus is systemic, preventive, and collaborative (Kronick 2005). Agee saw schools where the souls of the children were attacked, and the teachers were exhausted. Views of schools continue to vacillate today in their perceptions by all stakeholders.

Roger Guy (2019) states that hillbillies are an abstract caricature rather than a distinct culture or cultural type. For the children of Appalachian migrants whom I interview (Roger Guy) having roots in the hills of Appalachia primarily meant an identification and appreciation for unique expressions of art, music, and family, and a deep attachment to the land (Home, C p. 99).

Art, Science, and Value

The reader at this point may be wondering how Agee and Evans doing their work to understand man as Agee put it in their 1936 trek to Hale County, Alabama is relevant and adds to the understanding of people where they live, work, and play by scholar activists in 2020. Scholar activists today include J. D. Vance, Matthew Desmond, Alice Goffman, Casey Cep, and Colson Whitehead. The work of these scholars is qualitative and subject to all the pitfalls of this type of work. Vance's work has earned the ire of many scholars of Appalachia. The scorn he has received revolves around "Is he an Appalachian? Is his work generalizable? Is Ohio a suitable locale for the work?" In *Appalachian Reckoning,* the authors strongly attack Vance on these points. These authors see Vance's neo-liberal work as pandering to Donald Trump and victim blaming. Vance gives ample credit to his grandmother mamaw, but in his development of a paradigm for Appalachia and Appalachians, mamaw is not in the equation.

Matthew Desmond's *Evicted* (2017), a Pulitzer Prize winner in 2018, gives his insights into doing the work in Milwaukee, dictating his notes while walking around with his infant child. His findings that single black moms with children were those most often evicted in civil court where landlords with attorneys on retainer always won against tenants who were not guaranteed counsel. Desmond brilliantly describes a landlady who clears $100,000 a year and vacations in Jamaica. At the same time, he describes and analyzes a man who lost both his legs from frostbite while sleeping in a rental unit in Milwaukee. Alice Goffman in *On the Run* has written an en vivo account of criminal behavior. She lived this experience while writing this viable tome. Some scholars have even asserted that Goffman aided and abetted some who were on the run from the law. This book is a fine addition to the literature on criminology, yet Dr. Goffman was denied tenure at the University of Wisconsin and asked to leave the University of Ponoma. Alice Goffman is of further interest to engaged scholarship as she is the daughter of notable scholar Erving Goffman, who wrote

Asylums: The Presentation of Self in Everyday Life, Stigma, and others which provide useful theory to scholar activists.

SOCIAL SCIENCE AND THE ARTS

Social science is the mechanism by which we come to construct meaningful understandings of what is going on cognitively and behaviorally in the natural environment of individuals, groups, and communities. I believe that the Chicago School of Sociology, Mead, Cooley, Thomas, and others have provided some of the most valuable theory to those who want to understand day to day life of folks to the fore. Phenomenology makes us aware of the importance of understanding behavior from the quiet view of the actor (Husserl 1900).

Chapter 2

ON MAKING *LET US NOW PRAISE FAMOUS MEN:* A VALUABLE SOCIAL SCIENCE TOOL FOR UNDERSTANDING POOR PEOPLE AND POVERTY

"Looking is harder than it looks, because looking is not innocent"
-    Baldwin Lee

This chapter was part of the University of Tennessee's focus on poverty for the academic year 2009-2010. The University Assisted Community School Program was invited to participate in this event. Good publicity helps the project. The UACS at the University of Tennessee is constantly struggling for visibility and community and university support. This chapter was originally presented to a group of people who came out on a rainy January 2010 night, James Agee being from Knoxville was of interest to the group. Most of the audience had not thought of Agee's work as social science. Agee himself said it was not a book on social science; in fact, he said it was not a book at all.

The book, along with Baldwin Lee's work, is an excellent example of how outsiders connect with insiders; this is what service learners do in going into vulnerable schools where their background is different from those they are going to serve. Students from the University of Pennsylvania whom I observed at Sayre High School clearly overcame class differences in their serving. Students in the University of Tennessee UACS are doing the same. One of the ways this issue of class differences is handled is by having students examine their own culture as they begin their service-learning journey in a University Assisted Community School. Differences of race and class are a constant source of concern for service learners in a community school. Agee and Evans are stunning examples of this issue. Baldwin Lee (2010), a student of Walker Evans, is a master of connecting with people on their turf who are different from himself.

The following pages are designed to help the reader learn from the lived experiences of three families from Hale County, Alabama: southern, rural, poor black folks and the painter Joseph Delaney.

In a sense, this chapter should help all who want to work in an environment such as a community school where understanding culture, cultural difference, and cultural tensions is important.

"There are two fallacies that despite having been subjected to frequent criticism continue to inform the quest for more or better knowledge about the poor:

1. That good social science is a necessary apolitical ideologically or value-free endeavor;
2. The other that scientific knowledge about the poor will yield a rational scientific cure" (O'Connor, 2001 p. 22)

"We were not by any means at ease with each other. But he felt he could trust me and we liked each other." (Agee & Evans, p. 202)

Chapter 2

ON MAKING *LET US NOW PRAISE FAMOUS MEN:* A VALUABLE SOCIAL SCIENCE TOOL FOR UNDERSTANDING POOR PEOPLE AND POVERTY

"Looking is harder than it looks, because looking is not innocent"
- Baldwin Lee

This chapter was part of the University of Tennessee's focus on poverty for the academic year 2009-2010. The University Assisted Community School Program was invited to participate in this event. Good publicity helps the project. The UACS at the University of Tennessee is constantly struggling for visibility and community and university support. This chapter was originally presented to a group of people who came out on a rainy January 2010 night, James Agee being from Knoxville was of interest to the group. Most of the audience had not thought of Agee's work as social science. Agee himself said it was not a book on social science; in fact, he said it was not a book at all.

The book, along with Baldwin Lee's work, is an excellent example of how outsiders connect with insiders; this is what service learners do in going into vulnerable schools where their background is different from those they are going to serve. Students from the University of Pennsylvania whom I observed at Sayre High School clearly overcame class differences in their serving. Students in the University of Tennessee UACS are doing the same. One of the ways this issue of class differences is handled is by having students examine their own culture as they begin their service-learning journey in a University Assisted Community School. Differences of race and class are a constant source of concern for service learners in a community school. Agee and Evans are stunning examples of this issue. Baldwin Lee (2010), a student of Walker Evans, is a master of connecting with people on their turf who are different from himself.

The following pages are designed to help the reader learn from the lived experiences of three families from Hale County, Alabama: southern, rural, poor black folks and the painter Joseph Delaney.

In a sense, this chapter should help all who want to work in an environment such as a community school where understanding culture, cultural difference, and cultural tensions is important.

"There are two fallacies that despite having been subjected to frequent criticism continue to inform the quest for more or better knowledge about the poor:

1. That good social science is a necessary apolitical ideologically or value-free endeavor;
2. The other that scientific knowledge about the poor will yield a rational scientific cure" (O'Connor, 2001 p. 22)

"We were not by any means at ease with each other. But he felt he could trust me and we liked each other." (Agee & Evans, p. 202)

On Making Let Us Now Praise Famous Men   21

"It is simply an effort to use words in such a way that they will tell as much as I want to and can make them tell of a thing which happened in which you have no other way of knowing." (Agee & Evans p. 12)

"The school day means boredom for the students and exhaustion for the teacher." (Agee & Evans p. 67)

"This book had a resurgence in and rebirth in the 1960s with the election of John F. Kennedy and all that the '60s were about." (Kronick 2019 p. 52)

"What are writers trying to do? They're trying to create a universe in which they have lived or would like to live. To write they must go there and submit to conditions which they may not bargain for. Sometimes as in the case of Jack Kerouac the effect produced by a writer is immediate as if a generation were waiting to be written." (Burroughs p. 36)

Obviously, this is true of James Agee and Walker Evans's *Let Us Now Praise Famous Men.*

I will begin my discussion of *Let Us Now Praise Famous Men* as an excellent source of qualitative research techniques, which Agee and Evans claim it is not, with a phrase from the end of their book, "Whatever facts a person writes have to be colored by his prejudices and biases." This is an excellent beginning point for the experienced as well as the beginning field researcher.

Elliot Eisner and Robert Nisbet have built social science paradigms that are based on the principles of art. According to Eisner, art does the following in creating a social science structure:

1. Makes the obscure vivid and makes empathy possible.
2. Directs our attention to individuality and locates, in particular, what is general or universal.

22 *Robert F. Kronick*

Dorothea Lange's work is an excellent example of this concept. Her *Migrant Mother* is a well-known photograph that supports this contention.

3. Possesses a sense of wholeness and coherence, a kind of organic unity that makes both ascetic experience and credibility possible (152).

Art brings something into existence. A piece of clay becomes an ash tray, an idea becomes a photograph. Art has a valuing quality: standards are set; the contemporary piece is compared to the masters, Van Gough, Evans, etc. Art is a medium as is music, literature, and photography. In *Amazing Grace,* Jonathan Kozol (1995) describes Mrs. Washington's health. She has HIV and is making her own bed at the hospital after waiting there three days. Kozol's description of the hospital shows and compares with Agee and Evans's description of sharecroppers' houses. Mrs. Washington waits as long as she possibly can to go to the hospital so she will not have to pay. This allows her son to have more money when she dies. Kozol's work is inductive, descriptive, and designed to lead social action.

Eisner's imaginative exploration provides the material through which new perspectives are made available. Facts are made meaningful and coherence is made possible (p. 153). Robert Nisbet has referred to sociology as an art form. He quotes Herbert Read:

"The essential nature of art will be found neither in the production of objects to satisfy practical needs, nor in the expression of religious or philosophical ideas, but in its capacity to create a synthetic and self-consistent world...a mode, therefore, of envisaging the individual's perception of some aspect of universal truth. In all its essential activities, art is trying to tell us something; about the universe something about nature, about man, or about the artist himself." (1976, p. 10)

On Making Let Us Now Praise Famous Men
23

Frederick Moffatt (2009), in his biography of Joseph Delaney, describes Delaney's search with a companion to find a house from his youth in Virginia. Delaney and his friend set out on a search for the homestead but become diverted. To this point, the odyssey recalled the night he and Buford, his brother, had taken a walk in Pulaski. The one difference was that at that time in my youth, all of nature was a paradise, void of any discrepancies (Moffatt, p. 205). This sentence reflects how, in over forty years of painting, Delaney saw the world. Whether it was a Macy's Day Parade or a parade celebrating the Brooklyn Dodgers or figures of women, Delaney's upbringing in a Southern home headed by his preacher father influenced what he painted. His work took a strong span of what he thought was right or wrong. How interesting that both Agee and Delaney were born in Knoxville, Tennessee, but spent a major portion of their lives in New York City. Delaney painted urban scenes, whereas Agee had several works that focused on the rural south.

This next quote from Gabo, an artist, is in concert with symbolic interactionism: a major school of thought within sociology and a major underpinning of social psychology:

> "With indefatigable perseverance, man is constructing his life, giving a concrete and neatly shaped image to that which is supposed to be unknown and which he alone through his construction does constantly let be known. He creates the images of the world. He corrects them and he changes them in the course of years or centuries." (Nisbet 1976 p. 13)

The artist is interested in problems that are presented by reality and by the world of scientific fact (p. 18). This is the *raison d'etre* of social science and attempting to understand human behavior.

This chapter was stimulated by the University of Tennessee's focus on poverty for the academic year of 2009-2010. A focus on poverty is different from a focus on poor people. Up until this time in America, we have done more research on poor people than poverty itself. This is for a variety of reasons. The simplest being poor people can be blamed for their condition. It can be argued that poor people are poor because of internal reasons related to them only. Poverty on the other hand involves not only the poor but the non-poor. Poverty remains a fact of life for millions in the world's most populous economy and stubbornly resistant to what social scientists have learned about its causes and consequences and cures (O'Connor 2001 p. 3).

As knowledge on poverty became more about poor people and less about culture or political economy, the questions became more oppositional. The question became about money or culture (O'Connor 2001 p. 16). The issues revolved around opportunity structures versus personal motivation.

ENTER AGEE AND EVANS

A return to Hale County, Alabama, in the summer of 1936 helps to answer these questions and to throw light into the darkness. Agee & Evans (1940) give a brilliant insight into the life of three rural, poor families during this time. I am about to propose that *Let Us Now Praise Famous Men* is a fine piece of social science research, though Agee cogently states that this is not a book about social science. He asks the reader to not think of it as a book at all. Yet, he also says this is a book about sharecroppers. He declares strongly that "if complications arise, that is because they are trying to deal with it not as journalists, sociologists, psychiatrists, priests, or artists, but seriously" (p. XL VII).

The reality of being poor is not that one has nothing but rather has alternative versions of the things everyone else has. Being poor doesn't mean washing clothes by beating them against a rock at the river. The poor have a washing machine, but its motor is broken (Lee, np forthcoming).

"Let Us Now Praise Famous Men is the most assigned least read book in college" (personal communication with Mike Lofaro, December 15, 2009).

Lofaro said this was so because the book is so difficult to read. I find the book to be in line with many others that fall under the category of qualitative research narrative and ethnography. All of this would make Agee gag. A prime example is his thick, rich description of these three families, including their homes, clothing, and lifestyle. Agee implores us to tell and seek the truth; that there should be no form of fabrication. For truth to come out, for the words to tell the reader what he or she doesn't know, there must be correspondence between what is said and what is the case. Agee states in a letter to the Father Flye that "the whole problem and nature of existence" is what the Alabama project is all about (p. XXI).

WALKER EVANS AND BALDWIN LEE

"You just can't go up to somebody's house and say "I wanna come in and live here" (Agee & Evans 1940 p. XVI). "Down in front of the courthouse Walker had picked up talk with you" (p. 361).

"When I arrive in town, my first stop is the local police station where I announce that I am a tourist interested in taking photographs with very expensive camera equipment. The officers usually produce a map and red line those areas to be avoided. These are almost always where there is a concentration of black Americans. The red lined areas are where I go to make photographs" (Lee 2010).

After a while, Fields invited Evans and Agee to his house, and there at last, both knew they had found what they were looking for. They won the trust of all three families, eventually telling them exactly what they were up to and the families wholeheartedly accepted them (Agee & Evans 1940 p. 16).

26 *Robert F. Kronick*

In qualitative research, gaining entrée is the critical first step. Trust is a key facet of this process, and Agee, Evans, and Lee are able to do this. They have gained and do gain trust and build a rapport with people. A few stories will exhibit this most difficult phenomenon for the incipient writer and social scientist. The reader should not be fooled into thinking this is a simple process by the beautiful manner in which these photographers and writers describe it.

Agee believed and clearly stated that his views could influence what he wrote. But he found the perfect position to study and write about the three families – he lived with them. He stated, "the effect is to recognize the stature of a portion of unimagined existence and to contrive techniques proper to its recording, communication, analysis, and defense" (p. 46). Agee saw the families as good and used this to rail against a system that he saw as unjust. His comments on education are especially critical. He did not see the educational system as being able to help these folks in any way, shape, or form. His moral philosophy was one of anger against wrong and injustice. He fought to be true to his words, but he was totally true to these families. Yet, he wanted the book to tell everything possible and to invent nothing. His roots did help him empathize with the lives of the people in Hale County, Alabama.

The fact that the families felt a sense of loss when Agee and Evans left shows how strongly they fit with their subjects. They don't want them to leave. Yet Agee agonizes when he laments, "if I were not here; and I am an alien, a bodyless eye; this would never have existed in human perception. It has none. I do not make myself welcome here" (p. 187).

"I want you and Mr. Walker to know how much we all like you; we don't have to act any different from what comes natural to act" (p. 67).

Social researchers, especially those of a qualitative nature, should take a stand on how their research subjects feel or should feel as they do their work.

On Making Let Us Now Praise Famous Men 27

JAMES AGEE AND BALDWIN LEE

Description is central to *Let Us Now Praise Famous Men* and *In Consideration of Photographing in the South,* and qualitative research is general. Agee goes to considerable lengths to describe people, places, and things. He often reminds the reader to return to Evans's photographs as he or she reads through the book. I'm going to present here Agee's description of Emma.

"I am fond of Emma and very sorry for her, and I should probably never see her again after a few hours from now. He is a big girl...sexually beyond propriety to its years. Emma's very fond of her father and very sorry for him" (Agee & Evans 1940 p. 59).

"Emma loves good times, and towns and people her own age, and he (her husband) is jealous and mean to her and suspicious of her...and she can't have fun with anyone else because she is married and nobody will have fun with her that way" (p. 60). Emma is seen as sexual by Agee and others. Often this intimacy is a casualty in helping relationships and qualitative research.

"Each of us is attracted to Emma both in sexual immediacy and as symbols or embodiments of a life she wants and knows she will never have; and each of us is fond of her and attracted toward her. We are not only strangers to her, but we are strange, inexplainable, beyond what I can begin yet fully to realize (Agee & Evans 1940 p. 60-61).

Agee sees how Emma is trapped. She is married to a man who treats her poorly and in common parlance today we would say "has issues." At the same time, she dislikes her father's second wife. Agee uses intimacy, excitement, flirtation, and sensuality to describe his and Evans's feelings toward Emma. But he warns that neither she nor they can ever act on these feelings. He says, "there is a pleasure in all of this that no one would restrain or cause, yet there is also an essential cruelty about which nothing can be done" (Agee & Evans 1940 p. 60-61).

28 *Robert F. Kronick*

A question that arises here is whether students of the human conditions such as Agee, Evans, or Lee are insiders or outsiders when doing this type of work.

Baldwin Lee (2010) describes his people, places, and things eloquently. As with Emma, I will discuss only one of Lee's personal subjects, Robert Fulton. Some of what I write comes from Lee's proposed book and some from conversations I've had with Baldwin over thirty years. Compare how Lee meets Robert Fulton with how Agee and Evans connected with the Gudgers, Rickets, and Woods. "I pulled over and got out of the car and with my camera and tripod on my shoulder walked underneath the arbor and knocked on the door. A thin shirtless black man opened the door. I apologized for my forwardness and told him the goat and wisteria were irresistible to a photographer. He introduced himself as Robert Fulton." Remember Walker Evans said you just don't go up to somebody's house and say, "Hey I wanna come in and live here." Now a photograph versus living there are different, nonetheless the initial conversations required are similar (Lee 2016).

"The rollercoaster landscape resulted from the runoff of water from years of violent summer downpours. Upon closer examination I saw that significant efforts had been made to lessen deterioration of the land. Fight erosion was Mr. Fulton's self-appointed mission...the amount of work was herculean. It occurred to me to ask Mr. Fulton if he owned the land. He replied no. I asked why he worked so hard on another's property. 'God put this land here and God put me here, that's why I work' he answered" (Lee 2010). The story of Mr. Fulton is one of the first Lee shared with me and my students in a qualitative research course several years ago. I remember the visual that I had when Mr. Fulton explained to Lee why he put tires into the land to prevent erosion and that even though he didn't own the land God put him there to take care of it. Secondly, Lee sent Mr. Fulton a photograph. Mr. Fulton sent Baldwin some money, $5 I think. Baldwin contemplated sending

On Making Let Us Now Praise Famous Men   29

another photograph, but was convinced by his wife, I think, that if he did, more cash would follow.

Other subjects that Lee describes in thick rich detail are how tv sets are placed on top of another when they no longer work become pieces of furniture, cornflake boxes with pictures on them kept Mrs. Fulton company at meal time because her children had moved away and she wanted company when she ate. Lee also was asked to film a dead child by her parents, a resident who packs a gun in a homemade holster because his neighborhood isn't safe, and a man whom Baldwin helped get money to which he was entitled and then used it to drink himself to death, are discussed thoroughly. When Baldwin returned, the man's neighbor told him that he (Baldwin) bore responsibility for the man's change in behavior.

Agee goes to great pains to describe clothing, houses, and odors. Lee states the pragmatic purpose of clothing, protection from the elements, has evolved to include haute couture, where utilitarian function yields to the condition of being art. Clothing contains signals of gender, age, sexual preference, religion, and occupational categories, social and economic status. These signals allow us to not only differentiate but also prescribe the attitude and demeanor that should be assumed while interacting with those individuals (Lee 2010). Barbara Ehrenerich in *Nickel and Dimed* (2003), makes this point when describing her time working as part of a crew that cleans houses: her shirt marginalized her when she went for a coke at the convenience store.

Agee describes clothing along an aesthetic utilitarian continuum. Shoes are for work. Women wear their shoes when men wear them out. Clothing, especially for women, is made of fabric that wasn't its primary purpose. Dresses are often made of flour sacks. They are fitted especially for breastfeeding, coming down to a low V at the level of the line of the breast. Hats, in particular for Negroes where creativity may come into play, were especially important.

Clothing, as noted by Agee and Robert Coles, is often shared, especially by the children and especially the girls. Attendance at school may be determined by who has the clothing for that day. I have found that, in 2009, sisters will take turns going to school so that they may take care of one another's babies, a far cry from having to share clothing but certainly a picture of how things have remained too much the same for poor people.

Education is not seen as being very helpful to the sharecroppers of Hale County, Alabama, by Agee. He describes the school day as one of boredom for the children and exhaustion for the teacher (p. 294). Agee continues with thoughts that predate educational theory of the 1960s when he avers that "in school, a child is first plunged into the hot oil bath of the world at its cruelest: and children are taught far less by their teachers than by one another" (p. 311). Beginning in the 1960s, educational theorists placed a great deal of emphasis on self-concept and its relationship with learning. The consensus was that there was a strong correlation between positive self-concept and learning. A great deal of emphasis was placed on developing a child's positive self-concept. Sadly, the results weren't there. Possibly, the time order was the reverse: that good grades, an indicator of learning, led to a positive self-concept, rather than the other way around. I wonder if Agee read John Dewey.

Agee continues this line of thought with the following quote, "As a whole, part of psychological education needs to be remembered that a neuroses can be valuable; also that adjustment to a sick and insane environment is of itself not health but sickness and insanity" (p. 310). Both of these concepts are well-documented in the mental health literature, with the former romanticizing mental illness and creativity and the latter the social creation of mental illness. Van Gogh was often cited as an example of genius, creativity, and neurosis. He may also have had a brain tumor. Friedrich's (1975) *Going Crazy* described many cases of neurosis in genius ranging from bass player Charles Mingus to artist Vincent Van Gogh and composer Robert Shuman.

On Making Let Us Now Praise Famous Men   31

Thomas Szasz is a major proponent of the social creation of mental illness and the influence of labeling theory in the careers of mental patients. There is no question that adapting to a toxic environment is sure sign of mental illness. Students adapt to school environments for good grades. Historically, girls have done this quite well.

The Ricketts (p. 303) are an excellent example of how the school system casts a wide net that labels families and children. "They are spoken of disapprovingly even so far away as the county courthouse as 'problem children.' They often don't come to school and when they do come, they frequently sass the teacher" (p. 305).

I find this paragraph from Friedrich supportive in tone and method to Agee, Evans, and Lee. Friedrich's work moves this paper into social science research on mental illness. He uses a convenience sample method to gain access to his subjects who at one time were mentally ill and are now well enough to reflect on their psychiatric experience. He says, "I never tried to diagnose their anxieties, never argued with them. I was only trying to find out what they themselves thought had happened to them. And I was struck by the candor with which they spoke. They hardly ever used the euphemistic language of psychiatrists and social workers. They scorned such terms as 'inappropriate behavior' and 'character disorder.' They generally speak with a kind of embarrassed honesty of having been nuts or out of my mind" (p. 349).

I find Agee and Evans speaking at the courthouse with the Gudgers, Ricketts, and Woods, and Lee's impromptu visit to Robert Fulton's home congruent with Friedrich's open-ended questions to his formerly mentally ill friends. Notice he asks them "what" not "why." "What" facilitates conversations whereas "why" puts individuals on the defensive as these types of questions are blaming in nature.

Those who have lived the experience, rural poor, poor blacks, and mental patients at one time seemed to have a more earthly and concrete understanding of their condition that those who may be seen as experts or who work with them. Agee makes this a theme throughout the Alabama project. He is keenly aware of who the experts are in

32 *Robert F. Kronick*

Cookstown, Alabama. One is left to wonder why the Gudgers, Ricketts, and Woods did not go mad.

AGEE, EVANS, AND LEE—LITERATURE AND PHOTOGRAPHY AS ENTREES FOR LEARNING ABOUT HUMAN BEHAVIOR

To further the understanding of rural poverty in 1936 Hale County, Alabama gives insights into the three families, his family of origin and himself. Sex, violence, and faith are driving forces in Agee's life. He is drawn sexually to Louise, Emma, and Ivy.

> "Suddenly, yet very quietly, I realized a little more clearly that I am probably going to be in love with you (p. 369). All this while something very important to me is happening and this is between me and Louise. I come soon to realize that she has not once taken her eyes off of me since we entered the room." (p. 400)

His sexuality is expressed toward Louise, Ivy, and a whore he sees in a gas station on his short trip an intermission to Birmingham. He says I realized I needed and wanted a piece of tail. Standing naked in the night to escape the bugs at the Gudgers is also a moment of sexuality.

Violence is exemplified on the trip to Birmingham when Agee encounters three young boys and fantasizes what a fight with them would be like. He realizes that he would lose to any one of them, but the idea of a fight with them fascinates him. Like with the whore at the gas station, the fight with the three boys does not move beyond the idea of it. His faith in which he is not a true believer still runs constantly through his life. He avers that he is or was born a Catholic but believes in Communism.

As states earlier, Agee describes in thick, rich detail as qualitative research demands today. His description of houses, odors, and clothing

On Making Let Us Now Praise Famous Men 33

presented earlier is here discussed through a night he spent in bed at the Gudger's home, driving Gudger to the field to work, and getting his car stuck in the mud. I present these in abbreviated form. All of these events shape Agee's reporting of them because he lived them.

> "I began to feel sharp little piercings and crawlings all along the surface of my body. I lay a while rolling and tightening against each new point of irritation, amused and curious how I had changed about bed bugs (p. 4-5). Continuing on, I don't exactly know why anyone should be happy under these circumstances…I was outside the vermin, my senses were taking in nothing but a deep night, unmediatable consciousness of a world which was newly touched and beautiful to me" (p. 428).

The ride to Gudger's workplace the next morning after the description of the bed bugs is equally descriptive as Agee's fight with these bugs and vermin that he knows he will not win. After Agee and Gudger get the car out of the ditch, Agee describes in Gudger's dialect how to get from the car that is stuck to the fields where Gudger will work that day and many more days afterward.

CONCLUSION

I end this odyssey with Agee, Evans, Lee, and Delaney with a hope that through interdisciplinary action oriented work we will begin to understand human behavior and the human condition in such a way that interventions with poverty and poor people will be much more successful in the eyes of all concerned. A greater understanding on the storyteller's properties of research allows the other to concentrate on the ways in which texts reflect social reality (Hollis & Colyer, 2009). I hope this chapter aids in this endeavor I know Agee, Evans, Lee, and Delaney do.

Agee and Evans end their Alabama project with allusions to death when they state, "Until at length we too fall asleep." I will conclude with the beginning it also is a beginning for Agee and Evans when discussing words and photographs (remember that Agee and Evans are coauthors of *Let Us Now Praise Famous Men)* as they say and illustrate the importance of their collaboration. "I believe, too, that photographs are a true interpretation. One photograph might lie, but a group of photographs can't" (p. 453).

The academic community exists because of the mutual exchange of stories among its members (Nash 2004 p. 2).

Chapter 3

COMMUNITY SCHOOLS: WHAT ARE THEY? IMPORTANT SCHOLAR ACTIVISTS SPEAK

In many underserved neighborhoods, children's limited opportunities are compounded by out of school barriers to learning including trauma induced by housing instability, inadequate healthcare, food insecurity, and more broadly racial animus. All conspire to limit the life chances of these vulnerable children. Typical school reforms are likely to position or blame these challenges as exogenous community-based factors rather than seeing the school and its community as a coherent ecology in which schools have a critical but not sole responsibility for teaching, learning, and social betterment (Jeannie Oakes 2019).

This provocative paragraph from professor Oakes alerts us to two powerful phenomena: 1. Schools cannot deal with school problems by themselves. This warns those who do the work that they must collaborate with others to make teaching and learning possible. 2. Non-curricular variables such as food, shelter, clothing, and mental health must be dealt with for students to grow and learn. Kronick (2005) adumbrated that a community school should have at its core systems theory, collaboration, and prevention.

Community schools depending on one's perspectives are characterized by variety or lack of consensus on what they are. Yet, according to Jeannie Oakes (2019), they are a powerful response to parochial distinctions that separate the potential of communities from the potential of children. The fact that children don't vote and don't have a political constituency has long explained how and why issues pertaining to children rarely have support that is necessary to get political, financial, and social involvement to make the issues impossible not to see. Seeing the problem is easy enough to do. All you have to do is look. Yet, we must keep in mind what noted photographer Baldwin Lee said about looking.

Oakes (2019) continues with a definition of community schools by stating that they integrate health and social support for children and families, they offer expanded learning time and opportunities, and they engage families and communities meaningfully in the life of the school.

The following is what the UACS in Knoxville, Tennessee has accomplished in ten years beginning October 4, 2010. Following Oakes above the following is what we have done:

- Medical care is provided by Clinic Vols undergraduates majoring in pre-health such as medicine and nursing. This is basic health care, but it helps kids who may have colds and flu, high fevers, or need someone to talk to. Mental health care is provided by graduate students in psychology, school psychology, and counseling and the local mental health centers. The latter is an example of agency collaboration and that community schools are a place and a system of relationships. Joy Dryfoos (1994) was the major proponent of onsite school clinics. They were an essential part of the model she called Full Service. She believed parents didn't miss work and kiddos miss school with health care provided onsite at school. With medical support, school-based clinics served the community. Our clinic has not been successful in serving the community. The Gardner School in Boston at one time had a full-service clinic open many nights and weekends that served the school and the community. Dental care is provided to the children through contractual agreements with a dental practice in the community by our UACS. The following vignette illustrates how well our collaborative relationship works with this dental practice. A fourth-grade girl who recently arrived from Africa arrived at our school. She was pleasant but extremely quiet. One day, a teacher asked the student if she could look inside her mouth. Upon doing so, she saw teeth and gums that needed immediate attention. The dentist agreed and extracted four teeth. Usually this requires a second visit. His comment was she could possibly die from such a condition. The following week, this young girl was swimming on a class field trip. As an aside, I wondered why no one along the way caught this potentially serious condition.

The most comprehensive community schools today seek to be social centers whose families come together to strengthen neighborhoods and civil society more generally as well as students and the people in these schools with collaborative approaches to leadership and practice (Oakes 2019).

The prime example of the school as a social center move in today's world is Darlene Kamine's systemic program. She is certainly the go-to person for comprehensive programs that do what Oakes describes and even more. I am fortunate enough to have edited a book due out in August 2019. Kamine has delivered a stellar job in her chapter on what she has accomplished over thirty years and continues to do currently. She was a keynote speaker on engaged scholarship at a conference I co-hosted at the University of Tennessee in the fall of 2018. We have been friends for several years, and we have visited each other's programs. I recommend those who want to raise the level of their programs to read Kamine's work, pieces about her work, and visit Cincinnati. Kamine's work reflects this summary paragraph from Oakes...community schools alone cannot overcome all problems facing poor neighborhoods—but they can connect children and families to resources, opportunities, and supports that help offset the harms of poverty, foster healthy development, and promote learning (Oakes 2019 p. XI). From this position, I return to an early entry I made in the *Encyclopedia of Education* in 2002. There is an old saying that the more things change, the more they stay the same. The following are some of what I said in 2002.

- A major question in K-12 education is if excellence and equity are possible simultaneously in schools. Funding is rarely sufficient to meet excellence and equity needs. From all appearances, funds go to talented and gifted or challenged youth and those students in the middle are too often ignored. With the rising tide of social justice, there is a plethora of interest and energy toward social justice. Social justice hence is a major plank of community schools. There is no doubt that currently social justice is front and center in our society. Some examples are 1. the number of children living in poverty going to K-12 schools hovers at 50%, and 2. there is an overabundance of black boys in special education and juvenile corrections. The situation is no better in adult corrections. Michelle Alexander's *The New Jim Crow: Mass Incarceration in the Age of Colorblindness* has awakened academics as well as the general public to the number of young black men in prison for minor drug offenses. James Forman Jr. in his Pulitzer Prize winning *Locking Up Our Own* points out that in his career as a public defender, the judge, jury, lawyers, and defendants were all black. He also notes that President Bill Clinton capitulated to the black bourgeoisie and signed a law that incarcerated these young male black offenders.

Convicted in the Womb is a phenomenal autobiography of the author's life as a young man on the streets of Philadelphia. He makes an indelible assertion when he talks about being in a juvenile facility, "I was exactly where I was supposed to be. My grandfather, father, grandmother, and mother were all incarcerated as juveniles." As he said, "I was convicted in the womb" (Upchurch 1996). All of the scholar activists have worked and written on social justice. There are others, but I find these very cogent.

- Student mobility from the onset of our UACS program has been a major target. The goal was to reduce the almost 50% rate as much as possible. In 2019, our mobility rate is 36%. Mobility is an important variable that strongly affects teachers' ability to teach and students' ability to learn. In our community, those families who move some make a tour of these schools during the school year. Twenty years ago, the main reason these families moved was because of bad drug deals. Currently, these families move because of the rent being due and their inability to pay. This is a problem in search of a solution. We ought to be able to work with this segment of the population. Matthew Desmond mentioned elsewhere in this text provides excellent discussion of those who are evicted. One of our principals said twenty years ago that we know more about migratory birds than we do migratory children. What we see here is a burgeoning problem of homelessness interfacing with community schools.

Homelessness is a problem in communities small, medium, or large. Our community has made investments in domiciles and day shelters for homeless people. The day shelters with bathrooms and tables and chairs has merely moved people further out on the perimeter road where they have been living. Providing affordable housing and livable wages may help some of this population.

Many of our readers want to start programs such as community schools. The following are principles that have worked for us or others in the community school network across the country:

- Get the support of the superintendent, principals, teachers, staff, parents, and other stakeholders who may be unique to this community. The university or other intermediaries are well-served to keep in mind that collaboration is the most effective way to get what all stakeholders would consider success. it is important to be vigilant regarding the cultural differences between universities and other entities such as schools. Luter & Kronick and Kronick & Basma (2017) are useful sources concerning these issues.

- In building the community school program, one of the first decisions to be made is the philosophy and operation of the program as school-based or school-linked. The UACS in Knoxville, Tennessee, is school-based. This decision was based on organizational theory, limiting the number of couples and observing what happened when the school day ended and the children were waiting to go to their after-school programs, this is coupling. What I saw and heard was children being yelled at. I knew that would not be part of any program I was in charge of. By being school-based, our program gives our kiddos a snack and programming begins. At the same time that we are running an academic enrichment program, we are also providing services through the school. Our goal is to provide services that are fractured and difficult to find throughout the community. The school ideally is a hub of services, a one stop shop. Various programs focus on schools or communities. Harkavy and The Penn Group, Jim Grim and the IUPUI Group, and Bob Kronick and the UACS in Knoxville are examples of schools that are community schools following the UACS model. Community centers in Cincinnati and Buffalo are famously successful community center programs. Darlene Kamine in Cincinnati and Henry Taylor in Buffalo have made significant contributions over time.

- A community school is a place and a system of relationships. It is exportable but not replicable. Building relationships with human service agencies including corrections, mental health, welfare, and housing is a must. Providing services in a non-stigmatizing fashion and environment is a hallmark of community schools. Kronick (2015) and Kronick, Luter, & Lester (2017) have researched, worked in, and written of these situations

- Hire people who work well with children and families. These teachers, childcare workers, must have empathy and a capacity to work with children who come from cultural, social, and economic backgrounds different from themselves. Our program does not confuse credentials with competence. Our staff is eclectic and ranges from a cooking teacher with a master's degree to two teachers with master's and doctorate degrees in physics and engineering. Program coordinators Karen Holtz at Pond Gap and Blaine Sample at Inskip Elementary Schools are excellent resources on selecting people to work in community schools.

- A clear policy for admission into the University-Assisted Community School is necessary as rarely are there sufficient slots to take all children who need the program. At the outset as I was designing the program, I selected grades, test scores, behavioral referrals to the principal, and mental health concerns.

Over time, a multidisciplinary team has come into play, and they select students based on the needs of the children and their families. This team illustrates how principals and program coordinators collaborate.

Community schools must have an intermediary and a program coordinator. An intermediary is an agency that runs the program. They may be nonprofits, libraries, United Ways, and universities. Since I am a university professor, the community schools I work with are University-Assisted Community Schools. The UACS model grew out of the early work of Joy Dryfoos. Her 1994 book *Full-Service Schools* is the seminal work in the field of community schools. The UACS model evolved from Dryfoos's work into the UACS model. The leaders of the movement are Ira Harvaky and The Penn Group, Jim Grim at Indiana University-Purdue, Karen Quartz at the University of California, Los Angeles, Bob Kronick at the University of Tennessee, and others. Henry Taylor and Darlene Kamine are supporters of the community center model. The University of Central Florida has assembled a thirteen-county model, and they certify these schools. Their funding and state support are impressive. At this writing, I don't know what their program does with the exception of some solid school clinics. Some schools have school and community clinics that are separate entities. The University of Central Florida model like Kamine in Cincinnati and Penn may be systemic leaders in the drive to create and sustain community schools on a broad scale.

Chapter 4

A NOVEL WAY TO EXAMINE SOCIAL SCIENCE QUESTIONS: CASEY CEP AND COLSON WHITEHEAD, FOLLOWING THE TRADITION OF JAMES AGEE AND WALKER EVANS

"All these years out of that school and he still spent a segment of his days trying to decipher the customs of normal people."
-    Colson Whitehead 2019 p. 190

Novelists, muckrakers, and idealists have at various moments written of the human condition and social times that helped shape their writings. Ida Tarbell, Charles Dickens,

All these early writers set the stage for authors such as Casey Cep and Colson Whitehead who are discussed here, and James Agee and Walker Evans who are thoroughly discussed in chapter 2. Writers like artists see and depict events uniquely and in ways different from the common. I present these authors both publishing powerful novels in 2019. Cep's *Furious Hours* and Whitehead's *Nickel Boys* present thoughtful and stunning material for social science. Their work is a guide for those wanting to study the human condition, gather data (information), and present it in clear, thought-provoking fashion. Agee and Evans present the lives of three families and their communities in Hale County, Alabama in 1936. Cep writes of murders, insurance scams, a white liberal lawyer, Truman Capote, and most powerfully Harper Lee, author of *To Kill a Mockingbird*. Cep along with Lee were masterful collectors of information and analyzing it meticulously. Cep not only helps readers understand behavior with thick, rich description similar to if not a model in qualitative research. Whitehead's style is different, but his novel is based on a real-world institution for boys in the northern Florida town of Marianna. His two main characters are amalgams of boys who were incarcerated over the years at the Dozier School. Both of these authors are current authors who have much to say to those who work qualitatively to learn about the human condition. I have no way of knowing if Cep and Whitehead have read *Let Us Now Praise Famous Men*, but the three are a powerful trio in beginning a solid literature review of gathering data and presenting it in an understandable fashion for moving beyond what they present. Their writings also provide a standard to reify current qualitative theories. What I am proposing is not likely to sit well with literary folk or social scientists. Nonetheless, Eliot Eisner and Robert Nisbet have made solid contributions to this interdisciplinary work. They are discussed earlier in the current text.

Cep and Whitehead look at the same subject but from different vantage points. Cep analyzes adult crime involving murders, insurance fraud, and the specter of Harper Lee. Cep details the murders committed by a well-known minister of his wives. In each murder, there were eerily similar modus operandi of each murder. The good reverend had taken out insurance policies on them. The reverend secured the services of a top-flight lawyer who got him acquitted of each of the murders. What his lawyer couldn't do was protect him from being shot and killed at his last victim's funeral. Ironically, the reverend's killer

A Novel Way to Examine Social Science Questions   45

was defended by his lawyer. He too was acquitted. All of this occurred in and around Harper Lee's hometown of Monrovia, Alabama. The criminal justice system and burial rights by race in a southern, Alabama town. Whitehead's book, albeit a novel, is based on true accounts of the Arthur Dozier School in Marianna, Florida. This book illustrates how challenged marginalized people, in this case young black boys who were labelled for who they were determined by race, class, and power. Their early institutionalization carried over into their later lives. *Nickel Boys* is about what can go wrong when institutions are run for staff benefits not for rehabilitation or habilitation if their early lives in the free world were not normal, which I might define as healthy, out of jail, and employed. Carl Upchurch's *Convicted in the Womb,* Michelle Alexander's *The New Jim Crow,* Erving Goffman's *Stigma,* and other standard criminal justice works inform this section of chapter 4.

Upchurch's tone is autobiographical and very informative regarding life in the streets. The streets for Upchurch were in Philadelphia. Upchurch's work predates Alice Goffman's *On the Run,* also created in Philadelphia. Her work is also discussed earlier in this text.

This quote from Upchurch is insightful as to his unique view of himself. His social creation of himself is insightful to students who want to understand the lifestyle of Carl Upchurch and the folks of his neighborhood:

> "I grew up believing I deserved society's contempt just because I was black. With each act of violence, disappointment, and rejection, each stabbing, each shooting, each fight and bitter word from my mother, each meal that was not provided, each time I had to go to school in dirty clothes, I retreated further into myself to a place of empty distress and growing anger." (Upchurch 1996)

This most impressive paragraph adumbrates that Carl saw his family of orientation, parents, grandparents, extended family, along with society at large to use his words convicted him in the womb. When

46 *Robert F. Kronick*

your family and society collide against you, social deviance including delinquency, crime, and mental illness is inevitable. What social scientists call socialization, Upchurch terms it niggerization, which he says begins in the womb and continues through generations. Labelling theory (Schur 1965) posits that more is learned about behavior by looking at the audiences who respond to the behavior than the actors doing the behavior. These audiences are society, significant others, and agents of social control. Schur contended that these audiences played powerful roles in the behaviors that society labeled and that individuals internalized. From a societal perspective, deviant behavior is that behavior that people so label. Significant others such as family, peers, even media creations either support the behavior which labels the individual as delinquent or mentally ill, or they don't support the aberrant or recalcitrant behavior which helps deter this behavior. Agents of social control such as social workers, counselors, or parole officers, take in societal and significant other factors in making decisions how to respond to and handle those folks who get labelled here. Fonny in James Baldwin's *If Beale Street Could Talk* and Elwood in Colson Whitehead's *Nickel Boys* are examples of those who become role engulfed by this process and never escape what they were born into. Too much of this is a self-fulfilling prophecy where these deleterious outcomes are socially created.

Upchurch rises above this draconian situation by making this powerful statement:

"I cannot forget those I served time with nor can I deny the enormous weighted responsibility I bear toward my brothers and sisters who are still behind bars. I want to unite them to provide them with a constructive non-violent voice to speak for their constitutional rights as prisoner citizens. I want them to understand the direct link between being black and poor in America, the direct link between prisons and housing projects. I want to help break the cycle" (Upchurch 1996 p.130).

This paragraph is full of further pages and hours of discussion.

A Novel Way to Examine Social Science Questions 47

How does one remember those they served time with when one would think they would want to forget the pains of imprisonment? Many inmates adapt to roles while incarcerated. These roles range from gang member to one who does his/her own time. Carl became a voracious reader. He said the best people he met in prison were Toni Morrison, Malcolm X, and James Baldwin. He even states that Shakespeare wrote for black people. The first book he read in prison was propping up a table.

Upchurch learned during his formative years that in school he was not in the top, but on the streets he was exceptional. This is all the more remarkable as he attended Earlham College and Ohio State University and wrote *Convicted in the Womb,* a most provocative work. The link between being black and poor is a correlation that needs intense study and action. Henry Taylor (2018) has written extensively on not using poverty as an excuse for not teaching poor children of color. For many years, scholars have struggled with the differences between poverty and poor people. From my perspective, poverty is a concept that can be manipulated by changing scores as to what makes one or a family poor. The poverty rate can be changed by raising or lowering dollar figures. Poor people are those who are living in this morass whether in rural Alabama in 1936 or a correctional school in Florida which operated unmonitored and unsupervised by the state. Upchurch further avers the critical link between race and housing. If as Michelle Alexander states that young black men are filling up prisons upon release, they may not qualify for supported housing, easily becoming homeless and at risk for issues of mental health and crime. There is no question that this prescient paragraph from Carl Upchurch underlies the systems theory of Parsons (1959) and Urie Bronfrenbrenner (1979) that permeate this book.

"I grew up believing I deserved society's contempt just because I was black. With each act of violence, disappointment, and rejection, each stabbing, each shooting, each fight that I witnessed, each bitter word from

48   *Robert F. Kronick*

my mother, each meal that was not provided, each time I had to go to school in dirty clothes, I retreated further inside myself to a place of empty distress and growing anger." (Upchurch 1996 p. 17)

Any student of human behavior should learn much about it by analyzing what Upchurch says above. First, he states that he deserved society's contempt because he was black. This is true of outsiders or marginalized folks who accept the label that is foisted upon them. What happens that outsiders accept the negative role proffered rather reject or deny this identity. Race and people of color are easily identified, and hence excluded from full participation in the fullness of American society. Turner and Elwood, two characters in *Nickel Boys,* both banter back and forth about them accepting the negativity of the staff at Nickel and society. The cultural and familial acts of violence, lack of food, shelter, and clothing all are factors that inhibit reaching one's personal goals. The following vignette illustrates what Upchurch boldly states. This story begins ten years ago when our student is in third grade. He was an athletic third grader with an infectious smile (I have a picture of him in my office). During this important year of school, especially for reading, our student Andy has his father arrested and sentenced to prison for seventeen years. His response was to punch out the wall in the gym. The program coordinator and I (the director) took him home from the school at 8:00 p.m., which is against the law. As was her usual, his mother had locked him out of the house. On a weekly basis, we sent Andy home at the end of our University-Assisted Community School Programs day with a large bag of food, also against the law. With these issues against him, Andy still matriculated to middle school and then on to high school He graduated on time with his class. But there is more. Andy was an above average football player and track person. I read the newspaper and noticed that he was not picked by any college whereas some of his teammates were. The program coordinator and I went to his high school to find out what was up. We discovered he was several hours short of the state requirement to graduate. We did

A Novel Way to Examine Social Science Questions   49

what we could and met with him. He did graduate, but football was no longer in the picture. I ran into him some time later and was surprised to see him back in town. Another year has passed, and his grandmother has called me. Time will tell what follows, the miracle of Andy is that he has made it from our K-5 program to high school graduate. All with no trouble with the law. We know virtually nothing about his life from 6th-12th grade. This is a glaring weakness in our K-5 program. So far and somehow, Andy beat the odds presented above by Carl Upchurch.

This vignette presents clearly that a longitudinal program where follow-up of elementary school students is possible. Most extended day programs run through elementary school only. An exceptional study on graduation rates from high school of those students who attended an after-school program was completed by Mary Walsh and her colleagues at Boston College. Walsh has a long history in educational research and program implementation. Her work at the Thomas Gardner School in the Allston-Brighton section of Boston to a statewide program in Massachusetts is exceptional and mammoth in importance.

Upchurch continues by saying, "I had been socialized at home under the most negative emotional conditions; as a result, my socialization in school felt like an insult to my culture and values. My teachers berated me for not being what I had not been taught to be" (Upchurch 1996 p. 17). Upchurch's experiences clearly illustrate the home/school culture conflict that exists in our society. As our country becomes increasingly diverse, we see the need to diversify our teacher cadre. In the rural-urban south where I live and have worked for 46 years, our teachers are increasingly white females. The gap between home and school culture was eloquently discussed by Robert Coles (1993) when he described his experiences with children in Appalachia as saying there was home language and school language and that they preferred home language. The same has been said of black culture and public schools. How interesting that Appalachians and African Americans share the same cultural conflicts with public education. The question is how to rectify this? This issue is at the core of social justice concerns. This issue moves the problem from the intellectual/abstract to the real and applied. Upchurch continually brings these thorny issues to the forefront for needed action. He was a scholar activist to his very core.

This vignette from Upchurch is a further example that has played out over several years in our program. Carl tells us of stealing cookies that were sold during the school day. The reason was that he didn't have twenty-five cents to pay for them. The heinous part of this story is that his teacher knew he didn't have the money. So when the cookies were missing, Carl was the obvious culprit. All this did was isolate Carl from his chums while in school. It also served to make Carl very street smart. This simple little act of not providing complementary cookies turns into a complicated trip to social deviance, in this case delinquency and crime. One of the deleterious outcomes that Upchurch reports from experiences with school figures leads to social isolation. We are all social animals and need social reinforcement. In this situation, reinforcement for negative behaviors is better than being isolated or ignored.

Posturing is presenting oneself as being tough. This styling is often a defensive posture to keep from being assaulted. I have seen this posturing for many years, and occasionally this behavior transfers into the school and community.

Upchurch was socialized to the values of South Street, his neighborhood. Being tough and incarcerated were at the core of his identity (Kronick & Thomas 2008).

This quote from Alice Goffman (2014) adds further detail to the writings of Upchurch and Whitehead. When a man is fearful of calling the police instead settles disputes with his own hands, this violence is secondary deviance – the additional crime a person commits because he has been labelled a criminal (Lemert 1967).

Is this a study of the wretched underside of neoliberal capitalist America? Despite the social misery and fragmented relations, we all search for community, a sense of belonging (A. Goffman 2014).

A Novel Way to Examine Social Science Questions 51

The mere act of observation can in fact change the object observed. This follows because at the scale of a subatomic particle, the act of shining light or photons on the object to observe or measure either a position or speed can be enough to move it to another position or state. Thus, each observer is a participant in creating what they perceive as reality. The observer and the observed become co-participants in co-creating a changing reality. The mere act of observation further narrows the illusion of the separateness of subject and object (Behrstock B. 2006 p. 40).

The Hawthorne effect derived from the Westinghouse studies found that workers who learned that they were being studied changed their behaviors. Lighting, comfortableness of the workplace had less impact on worker productivity than those who knew they were being observed.

W. I. Thomas cited that if a situation is defined as real, it is real in its consequences. Thomas claimed that the world was socially created through a world of subjective reality. Through symbols and referents, men/women create their world. These three similar ideas help us understand the world around us and how scholar activists go about learning what's going on. Michael Caine uttered what it's all about and Alfie and Marvin Gaye sang what's going on. Referents are what symbols refer to. They may be empirical or non-empirical. Symbols and referents are how we communicate. This approach in social science, most notably sociology, is the mechanism by which the Heisenberg theorem is applied to human behavior. And so here we are back to James Agee, Walker Evans, and Baldwin Lee. Hearing Agee's powerful voice uttering this is not social science but love. It's Barry Behrstock giving an intimate snapshot of glassblower Richard Marquis through his detailed and insightful look at Marquis the man, his wife Johanna, and their house/home cannot be separated. Behrstock citing the Heisenberg uncertainty principle makes clear that the observer and the observant cannot be separated.

DIFFICULTIES IN ASSESSMENT AND MEASUREMENT

The Godzilla in the room when it comes to assessing the effectiveness of interventional programs such as community schools is what are we measuring and how. The what is faced with how researchers and evaluators operationalize and define concepts. With community schools, it starts with how communities are defined and what indicators are good to operationalize the concept. Keep in mind that there is always a gap between the concept and the indicators.

We are in love with measurement and some would claim that if we can't measure it, it is not real or worth doing. At the same time, funders and government officials demand data. Is the program moving the needle as the current idiom puts it. The basic point is, is there predicted change associated with this program or intervention? Robert Martinson (1974) writing in criminal justice and studying treatment programs boldly stated that nothing works. Nothing works was in the title of this landmark study. Years later he recanted on his claim of nothing works.

Upchurch lives a very personal account of what works or what doesn't when he says, "Glen Mills taught me how to follow rules, but it didn't prepare me at all to go out and lead a moral, nonviolent life. If anything, I got tougher there, developed a bigger reputation, and became even more hardened to violence I saw and committed" (Upchurch 1996 p. 49). This scenario plays out in correctional schools and institutions across the country daily. Carl's utterances reify what Martinson states and what Colson Whitehead reported, albeit fictionally, in *The Nickel Boys*. He became prisonized (E. Goffman) where he followed rules but not much else. He even describes posturing which I have seen.

Chapter 5

THE PAST, PRESENT, AND FUTURE OF THE GOALS OF EDUCATION FOR ALL: SOME PERSONAL ASIDES

This chapter is an anthology of events expressing my thoughts, feelings, and actions beginning with the germination of the idea of what full-service schools are and could be. Ironically, I believe there was more consensus on definition of community schools.

Joy Dryfoos in her 1994 classic set the tone for what a full-service school was. Her choir mates Jane Quinn, formerly of Children's Aid, and Marty Blank, founding director of the Coalition of Community Schools continue this tradition (Ferrara & Jacobson 2019).

Dryfoos saw schools as community hubs where disorganized services could be brought together under one roof in a school which Dryfoos asserted is a piece of real-estate we all own. She believed that clinics in schools were a necessity. The full-service model was/is designed to meet the needs of the total child and their families.

(Personal note: through an incredible piece of luck I was on a panel with Joy at the 1998 American Educational Research Association (A.E.R.A.), and I was able to get her to come to Knoxville in late fall of

54

Robert F. Kronick

that year. This jump-started work I was doing independently of Dryfoos and her work.

HOW I GOT INTERESTED IN SCHOOLS

Before I met Dryfoos, I had worked in corrections and mental health. I found out one day that after spending several hours with three boys who killed a homeless person in a public park that I wanted to do prevention, and schools were the places to do it. I wrote my first book at that time (Kronick 2000). At the same time, I started a full-service school with the support of principal Blenza Davis. This was in January of 2000. Blenza and I are friends today. I had four schools running at this time with undergraduate students staffing these schools. These schools continued until 2010 when a generous donor gave us a grant that lasts in perpetuity. Other grants and awards from Dow Chemical, Krystal's Hamburgers, United Way, and 21st Century after school grants have made this UACS sustainable. Without sustainability, these programs may do more harm than good.

After this initial all-too-short meeting with Joy Dryfoos, she died. I had the next fortuitous meeting with Ira Harkavy and the Penn Group, Joann Weeks, Rita Hodges, Cory Bowman, and Linda Satchel who organized the first meeting with the Penn Group and a team I put together from the University of Tennessee. This eclectic group was comprised of the deans of Law & Education and Health & Human Sciences, a special assistant from the College of Education, Health, & Human Sciences, a colleague from the Howard H. Baker Center for Public Policy, and myself. This initial trip to the Netter Center at the University of Pennsylvania has been rewarding for me personally and professionally (I am writing this chapter in Philadelphia), but the University of Tennessee in 2019 is struggling with community engagement, and there is no support for a center such as what Penn has

The Past, Present, and Future of the Goals of Education for All 55

created. The interesting thing is that in the work in our schools continues to grow, and on September 6th we will showcase our outdoor classroom funded by Dow Chemical to the Colleges Board of Advisors.

Our colleagueship with the University of Pennsylvania Netter Center continues today and has led to professional relationships with Henry Taylor at the University of Buffalo, Gavin Luter at the University of Wisconsin, and Jim Grim at Indiana University at Purdue. Other scholar activists I have met through doing the work and who published chapters in books I have edited are William Conwill - University of Illinois, Mary Walsh - Boston College, Darlene Kamine - Cincinnati Community Centers Project, and Jane Quinn, current doctoral student and longtime advocate with Children's Aid. These are all folks who are seasoned scholar activists and program planners and developers who may contact and read about their work in your journey in becoming scholar activists.

THE JOURNEY 1966-1970

I left Florida in 1966 with a bachelor's degree in economics and psychology and entered the master's program in psychology and sociology at Appalachian State University in Boone, North Carolina. At that time, ASU had approximately 5000 students, becoming a state university, and jettisoning teacher's college from its title. Today, Appalachian State has some 25,000 students, and Boone and Watauga County have also grown. During this time, I became involved in a small way in the war on poverty and community action through a program called Youth Educational Services (YES) with other programs such as Congress of Religion in Appalachia (CORA), Save Our Cumberland Mountains (SOCM), Appalachian Volunteers, and Volunteers in Service to America (VISA). This was a time of optimism and hope. Most of us doing this work were not from North Carolina, but in true

56 *Robert F. Kronick*

Appalachian culture most of us developed a sense of peace and a true love for each other and the mountain people of western North Carolina. A few worth mentioning are Ray Hicks, the teller of Jack tales, Doc Watson, singer, guitarist, and much more, Noily Triplettt, postmaster of Triplett, North Carolina, and faithful reader of the Sunday *New York Times,* Wise Mains from Meat Camp, North Carolina who told me with a gun in his belt that they got my brother but they won't get me, and the Miller family who had seventeen children but who were clean when we came to tutor or go on a field trip to Tweetsie railroad. The Miller household had no running water or electricity during the time I was there. From here it was on to a doctoral program and in the fall of 1971 starting a human services department at the University of Tennessee.

The University of Tennessee Odyssey: Corrections, Mental Health and Education 1971-2019.

My arrival at university education which has lasted for the past forty years began in 1971 with the placement of students with the Department of Probation and Parole. This department was supervised by Stonney Ray Lane who later became warden of Brushy Mountain State Prison, home for a time to James Earl Ray, convicted killer of Dr. Martin Luther King Jr. Ray's capture is beautifully depicted by Lane in *Building Time at Brushy.* I return to Ray's capture later in this chapter. I learned a great deal about corrections from Lane that has helped with the people I work with. Corrections people are straight-forward, and of the three systems I have worked with, the easiest to get along with. In prison work, the count is most important. If the count is off, someone is missing. Security within the institution is critically important. The safety of the community is the third critical element of the system. The reader may want to reread Carl Upchurch and Colson Whitehead to learn how these viewpoints fit or not. Through mental health, I saw the workings of an avant-garde educational program developed by Nicholas Hobbs re-education. Hobbs claimed that children needed education not therapy. Hobbs believed that healthy living was healing. His concept of teacher counselors was based on the behavioral concept of modeling.

The Past, Present, and Future of the Goals of Education for All 57

Hobbs was a proponent of B.F. Skinner's work. It was in this environment that I started a group home for children who had committed delinquent acts but who could be in the custody of corrections or mental health. Once again, learning went on that influenced my work in K-5 education. I found early on that the number one need for children in Title I schools was for mental health care.

FULL-SERVICE COMMUNITY SCHOOLS 1999-2019

During this twenty-year period, I started the full-service community school idea, and in 2010 the model changed drastically with the infusion of money. This money has been used for the following:

- As a school-based program, staff had to be hired. Between two schools, we have 25 staff working various hours per week. All are University of Tennessee employees. They do the following: teach and tutor reading and math; science taught through a UT professor who has a million-dollar grant; art, music, dance, and theater are taught based on the availability of staff. Other courses that are purposeful to the curriculum and the UACS program are cooking, circus, gardening, and others that may arise through the special expertise of staff. A weekly curriculum devised by Karen Holst and Blaine Sample, program coordinators, is presented here. This is a schedule that has proved to be successful over the past several years:

58   *Robert F. Kronick*

Report to the Department of Educational Psychology and Counseling on Pond Gap and Inskip Community Schools Reviewing the 2017 – 2018

Prepared by:
Blaine Sample – Coordinator Inskip Elementary
Karen Holst – Coordinator Pond Gap Elementary

Overview

Pond Gap Elementary School (PGES) and Inskip Elementary School (IES) are both located in high-poverty, high-minority areas with 100% Title I students. Both are Knox County Community Schools (KCCS) which address student and familial needs through the provision or brokering of health services, mental health interventions, dental, basic needs, and other services that will minimize the distractions to learning in our students' lives. Through these key strategies, some new, and some enhancing our current efforts, PGES and IES provides a robust, personalized learning environment for each pupil that will enable and support academic success and eventual college and career readiness for all our students. The project design aligns to the community school adapted model and emphasizes five core improvement priorities: (1) academic learning, especially connections between in-school learning and learning during out-of-school time; (2) youth development, (3) parent/family engagement and support, (4) health and social services, and (5) community partnerships.

In recent years, we have seen an ever-increasing need and desire for after school activities, particularly around academics and unique physical activity and arts opportunities, for our students. Currently, through University of Tennessee's University Assisted Community Schools (UACS), UT students, faculty, and staff provide school

The Past, Present, and Future of the Goals of Education for All 59

children academic support services, physical education, music, and art programs after regular school hours from 2:30 – 6:00 pm daily at Pond Gap and 2:30 – 5:30 daily at Inskip. UACS is able to enhance the interpersonal skills, critical-thinking skills, and academic success of participating children. UACS creates challenging learning opportunities for students to excel by providing a nurturing environment supported by multiple sectors of both the Pond Gap and Inskip communites. These supports include families, community organizations, UACS staff, UT students, and UT faculty members. Collectively we are dedicated to increasing attendance and decreasing tardiness, increasing grades and academic performance, decreasing behavior referrals, and expanding community interdependence.

These community school sites are a positive center of influence that benefits students, families, and the surrounding community. Many unique programs are in place that uplift and enrich students' academic, social and emotional needs in order to help them become thriving and successful members of a healthy community. One of the initiatives is an after school-tutoring program. Current daily tutoring services are offered to targeted 1st through 5th grade students. Staff, administration and families recommend students based upon their academic, social, and emotional needs. These students receive tutoring services each afternoon in reading and math as well as homework assistance. After school teachers plan lessons that correlate with the skills that students are working on during the regular school day. We are able to meet students' needs not only through traditional academic methods, but also through enrichment programming and community partnerships. The UACS program at Pond Gap originated in 2010 as a 5 day a week program serving 40 students. The program has grown to serving 107 students in 2017-2018, 5 days a week from the end of the school day to 6:30pm. Inskip Elementary was added to UACS offering year-round programming in January of 2016. The growth of Inskip outstripped all predictions serving 120 students in 2017-2018. The demand for our services still exceeds ou capacity as we have a referral list of students waiting entry at both schools. While the UT after school services are invaluable to the students who participate, the current capacity does not meet the needs of all students and families that qualify for after school programming.

Program Description 2017 – 2018

At Pond Gap, hours of operation for regular programming are Monday through Friday after school from 2:30 – 6:00 pm. Snack and Structured Play are offered from 2:30 – 3:30 Monday – Friday. Tutoring classes are offered from 3:30 – 4:30 Monday – Friday and are designed to correlate with grade-level school wide goals and objectives for students having academic difficulty. A wide variety of enrichment classes are offered from 4:30 – 5:30 Monday through Friday. Enrichment programs provide a physical fitness and nutrition component for all students along with a rich variety of arts selections. Following dinner at 6pm, University of Tennessee students lead clubs up to 7pm.

Music enrichment at each site teaches the fundamentals of music while incorporating math, reading and writing into each lesson. The goal is that the students will develop understanding of music through experiences in singing, performing rhythms, moving to music, composing, and listening. Students develop the ability to read and notate music while also demonstrate understanding of the relationship of music to history and culture.

Art enrichment at each site includes key goals for every lesson taught. These goals are building self-esteem, inclusion, and the implementation of cross-curriculum materials. It is important that our students are not only able to create art that reflects their individual abilities, but to also gain a feeling of self-worth and pride. Additionally,

The Past, Present, and Future of the Goals of Education for All 61

by implementing math and reading into many of the art lessons, cross curriculum goals are met.

Language classes at each site are designed to teach students about the culture of the languages they are learning, including the culture of those who communicate with sign language. Expanding student's worldview enables them to be better prepared for the future. Foreign language study in the early elementary years improves cognitive abilities and studies show this exposure positively influences achievement in other disciplines.

Nutritional Programs and Physical Activity

We aim to promote a healthy and active lifestyle for youth. UACS offers physical activity in Circus Arts, Dance, Tennis Club, Soccer, Running Club, Gym Games, and Basketball Club. We have learned that the key to instilling healthy lifestyle habits comes in coupling fitness classes with a complete nutrition education program (Garden, N.E.A.T, and Cooking).

Dance classes including African and Latin Dance, provide an outlet for emotional and creative expression in a challenging, collaborative and supportive environment. Students learn the basics of traditional dances of two major world regions while reinforcing concepts taught during the regular school day. An attention to focus, practice, and improvement supports the social emotional wellness of students as they gain confidence and ultimately perform for a large audience.

Running Club also reinforces the health and physical fitness goals of the program. Participants in running club entered and completed a 5K race (the L.E.A.P. Race) on May 5 of 2018. This was a first for our students and five of our students won medals for their age group.

Tennis classes introduced students to the basics of Tennis and scholarship were provided through a partnership with individual donors to sponsor a Tennis Team for students to compete.

Basketball Club introduced students to the basics of basketball. Drills were presented in a fun and engaging manner which emphasize individual improvement and team values. Basketball Club along with all the fitness clubs mentioned above allowed our students to practice the virtue of hard work, self-discipline, self-improvement, and teamwork.

Circus Arts offers kids a chance to explore physical education through a unique lens. In circus class, we learn specific skills such as stilt walking, juggling, tightrope walking and unicycle. We also practice school-wide values like teamwork, communication and compassion. Circus class gives students an opportunity to practice building new skill sets in a safe and supportive environment. Children are taught that circus stands for **C**ooperation **I**nspiration, **C**onfidence, **U**niqueness, and **S**ocialization. Circus instruction not only provides children with a fun set of circus skills, but also provides them with important life-skills, such as patience with themselves and others, strength of character, kindness and emotional intelligence.

Cooking classes coupled with *Nutrition Education Activity Training* (N.E.A.T. offered in partnership with the Knox County Public Health Department), and *Garden Class* round out our programming to promote health and healthy active lifestyles for students.

Pond Gap has a thriving ¼ acre "Food Forest/Garden" that produces healthy, organic, nutritious food for our students, parents, and community. Inskip Elementary has also established a thriving school garden with booming production since its establishment. Both gardens serve as a hands on education hub for the current University Assisted Community Schools after school program with educational programs taught throughout the after school portion that use the garden as a hands on learning resource. The garden also hosts classes throughout the day, providing a supplemental resource for the curriculum or as an

The Past, Present, and Future of the Goals of Education for All 63

alternative educational asset. Crops produced are used in Cooking Club, and distributed among students and families. Community members also receive the produce from the garden through a seasonal food stand and through distribution in association with Knoxville Dream Center Food Truck.

Cooking Class is a new program at both schools. Students cook plant based meals engaging in every stage of the preparation and cooking process. This new club has impacted food choices in favor of healthy selections. Students harvest the food they have grown in the garden and transform healthy vegetables to tasty meals. Their direct involvement in preparing true farm to table meals instills a sense of pride and ownership that engages students in eating healthy foods. In conjunction with *Nutrition Education Activity Training (N.E.A.T)* classes, students are immersed in a full experience of nutrition education, healthy eating, and physical fitness all impacting positive health outcomes for our kids.

Additional enrichment classes offered through partners focus on STEM education and character/confidence building. In partnership with Boy Scouts of America, Pond Gap receives 20 scholarships for weekly *STEM SCOUTS* class for 5th graders. These hands on science and math activities fully engage students and ignite their passion for subjects that can be intimidating. *Girls Inc.* provides STEM focused programming weekly to Pond Gap and Inskip girls with a focus on building girl's confidence. *Lego Robotics* is offered through the University of Tennessee Haslam Scholars at each site and engages our students in the engineering aspects of Lego construction and also teaches programming skills as students turn their Lego creations into moving Robots.

Further, under a contract with KCS, the Helen Ross McNabb Mental Health Center provides services at each site to students identified as needing extra support in addressing youth mental health issues. UACS partnered with the UT College of Education, Health and Human Sciences to provide a Master's Degree student for mental health assistance. This non-clinical support includes behavioral strategies and de-escalation techniques for children struggling with anger management and impulsiveness as well as coaching and mentoring to increase self-esteem and decision-making.

An additional new feature at Pond Gap is a mentoring program called *"Boys to Men"* offered Monday – Thursday from 12:00 – 2pm. A male staff member works specifically with 50 boys in the school identified by the school intervention team. The mentoring program focuses on anger management techniques, making positive choices, and time for our boys to talk about the pressures they currently face. This program emanates from a need identified by both parents and school staff from open-ended survey data collected. We learned that partnerships to match students to mentors were successful for female students, however adult male mentor volunteers in partnering organizations were scarce. As a result, 90% of boys at Pond Gap waiting to be partnered with a male mentor remained unmatched by the end of a school year. The Boys to Men program has been highly successful and funding has been secured to continue this program for the 2018-2019 school year.

ACCOMPLISHMENTS AND REFLECTIONS

A primary focus for 2017 – 2018 school year for site coordinators Blaine and Karen centered on securing necessary funding for continued operation. Both Blaine and Karen partnered with Knox County Schools in writing and submitting grants to secure 21st Century Funding and each school was awarded funding. Both Inskip and Pond Gap now receive over $100,000 annually in 21st Century funding to assist in the operation of the after school programs at each school. Inskip Elementary had never received these funds. Blaine led the successful bid for this funding. The new grant award at Pond Gap represents a three-fold increase in funding over the monies received in the previous

The Past, Present, and Future of the Goals of Education for All 65

grant cycle. Karen relied heavily on the support of Blaine in securing a successful bid for these funds. These monies are critical as we now support two thriving Community Schools.

Additionally, through the leadership of Dr. Kronick, we were successful in securing a $375,000 United Way Grant to be administered over three years. These monies are especially important to assure the continued support of the vigorous program at Inskip Elementary.

Both Blaine and Karen engage in seeking out additional funding. Additional funding secured includes:

- Personal donations by Community Members to benefit Inskip Fine Arts Program
- Personal donations by Community Members to benefit the Pond Gap Cooking Club
- $2,400 award by Krystal to benefit the Pond Gap Cooking Club

Our funding efforts during the 2017-2018 school year highlighted the positive working relationship between Karen, Blaine, and Dr. Kronick. More than ever, we are working effectively as a team, recognizing our individual strengths and successfully leveraging those in achieving our goals.

Performance Goals

Goals: All students will reach high academic standards at a minimum attaining proficiency or better in reading/language arts and mathematics; All students will exhibit positive behavior changes that support academic and social growth; The percentage of students who are chronically absent from school will decrease; and, Family Engagement will be embedded in the entirety of the program.

Performance Goal 1: All Students Will Reach High Academic Standards at a Minimum Attaining Proficiency or Better in Reading/Language Arts and Mathematics

Performance Targets

1. At least 50% of all students who participate in the program for 30 days or more will have improved Math grades from fall to spring
2. At least 50% of all students who participate in the program for 30 days or more will have improved Reading/Language Arts grades from fall to spring
3. At least 40% of all students who participate in the program for 30 days or more will be proficient or above in Math on state assessment
4. At least 40% of all students who participate in the program for 30 days or more will be proficient or above in Reading Language Arts on state assessment

Activities

Each participating student is offered individualized homework assistance and tutoring (remedial education) in identified areas of need. Reading occurs daily and one hour will be dedicated to the academics of math, reading/language arts, and/or science for those struggling to become proficient. The academic time includes problem solving, project-based learning in fun and engaging modalities in which each student can relate. Foreign language is offered weekly through the University of Tennessee. By offering foreign language we are able to help our ESL students meet their academic goals. Computer time is part of the strategy for facilitating the learning of mathematics, reading, language arts, science and social studies. Activities vary by developmental appropriateness.

Professional Development

Teachers will receive 12 hours a year of professional development. Teachers will meet monthly for our "Pond Gap Brush Up" led buy the UACS director. Review of techniques, staff reflection of success and struggles, and adjustments in strategies to assure targeted performance goals of the grant are being met will be the focus of the monthly "Brush Up" sessions. The UACS director continuously encourages and assigns professional development through workshops and UT colleges.

Performance Goal 2: All Students Will Exhibit Positive Changes That Support Academic and Social Growth

Performance Targets

1. At least 75% of students who participate in the program for 30 days or more will have improved outcomes in timeliness and accuracy of homework completion.
2. At least 75% of students who participate in the program for 30 days or more will have improved classroom participation and classroom behavior.
3. At least 75% of all students who participate in the program for 30 days or more will have improved outcomes in relations with peers.

Activities

Homework help will be provided to students during before and after school hours. PBIS strategies will be implemented and reinforced during 21st Century learning time. Programs such as Girls Inc., Boys to Men Mentoring, Gardening and pro-social strategies are promoted throughout programming.

Professional Development

Teachers receive 12 hours a year of professional development. Teachers will meet monthly for our Pond Gap professional development designed to meet targeted areas of the grant. School wide PBIS training is offered to all Knox County Schools and UACS staff.

Performance Goal 3: The Percentage of Students Who Are Chronically Absent from School Will Decrease

Performance Targets

1. At least 75% of students who participate in the program for 30 days or more will miss 14 or fewer days of school each academic year.

Activities

Activities will be designed based on student needs. Interpersonal development between staff and students to determine student interests and to build relationships. Holistic problem solving as an intervention with students, parents, teachers and UACS staff.

Under a contract with KCS, the Helen Ross McNabb Mental Health Center provides services on site to students identified as needing extra support in addressing youth mental health issues. The service is provided during and after school hours.

Professional Development

Teachers receive 12 hours a year of professional development. Teachers will meet monthly for our Pond Gap Professional Development which is designed to meet targeted areas of the grant.

Performance Goal 4: Family Engagement Will Be Embedded in the Entirety of the Program

Performance Targets

1. At least 90% of all parents with children/youth who participate in the program will report that the program offers useful resources and materials such as workshops on homework assistance, parent advocacy, adult education classes, etc.
2. At least 90% of all parents with children/youth who participate in the program will report that there is always program staff available to discuss individual student needs.
3. At least 90% of all parents of children/youth who participate in the program will report that the program provides an open, welcoming environment for families.
4. At least 80% of parents with children/youth who participate in the program will report overall high level of satisfaction with the quality of provided services.

Activities

Parent surveys to inquire needs, strengths and disparities. Monthly parent engagement opportunities such as workshops, cultural events, health fairs and parent committees will be offered. A full time program coordinator is on site daily as well as KCS and UACS staff. The program coordinator has an open door policy with all-day office hours, public e-mail address and public phone number. Translation services are available though our partnership with the University of Tennessee. We employ a Swahili speaking staff member to link our families to school. We do this to improve our communication and inclusivity for families. All staff will work within their competency and professional credentials.

Professional Development

Teachers receive 12 hours a year of professional development. Teachers will meet monthly for our Pond Gap Professional Development which is designed to meet targeted areas of the grant. Full time staff participate in community wide trainings and workshops.

Partnership

The University of Tennessee has been working in partnership with KCS since 2000 and will continue to do so into the future. UTK provides employees: to work with the many community volunteers, to provide tutoring and mentoring services and evening dinner furnished by the KCS Food Services Department utilizing the free/reduced lunch program for underserved communities.

Further, this partnership will integrate and build upon existing activities and services provided to target youth as well as maintain functional communications to ensure appropriate student activities. The University of Tennessee as well as our many other partners recognizes the need to incorporate educational programs. We will not only help students meet and reach academic standards in core content areas, but will also help the students connect their academic achievement and personal life skills.

Organizations such as the Haslam Scholars Program, University Honors 267-honors service learning, Girls Inc., HABIT, Chi Epsilon, and the Knoxville Museum of Art among others have ensured their commitment to support programming at Pond Gap and Inskip Elementary UACS. In addition, UT UACS provides a site coordinator at Pond Gap and Inskip to ensure that this project is sustained and continues in the future. Pond Gap and Inskip volunteer support has continued to increase and there has been a multitude of community involvement within programming such as Keep Knoxville Beautiful,

The Past, Present, and Future of the Goals of Education for All 71

Pellissippi State Community College. CAC Green Thumb, the Arnstein Jewish Community Center, and Sequoyah Hills Presbyterian and First United Methodist Presbyterian Churches.

TO INFINITY AND BEYOND

As the leaves of fall approach in the foothills of the Great Smoky Mountains of East Tennessee, I begin a program that reminds me of *Back to the Future.* I will try my damdest to get a UACS embedded in a K-12 school in an isolated area northwest of Oak Ridge, Tennessee, home to some of the smartest people in this country. The community is home to 547 residents and the K-12 school has 400 students plus or minus in our initial visit to the school, which is K-12, the county mayor, two school administrators, and the principal and assistant principal met with the president of the university and myself from the University of Tennessee. The meeting served as an ice-breaker to see if this rural school and the UACS could work together in developing a university-assisted community school. The school has some programs in place, what it needs is some organization of these programs and the development of a seamless organization that wants to be open extended hours, days, and weeks. For example, the UACS program could be open 3-6 p.m. Monday through Friday possibly serving dinner and one Saturday a month with programs in science, arts, and culture. Get some local folks to show indigenous skills of the area. A summer program could provide academics so that the students don't fall behind or lose gains from the school year. These are beginning points, and the UT team will listen to the school people to what needs and assets are in place. A rural school may be a unique challenge to the field. Time will tell.

Chapter 6

HISTORICAL ANTECEDENTS: WHAT ROLES FOR UNIVERSITIES IN COMMUNITY CHANGE

If one really wants to understand something, one must try to change it. In the doing one learns, and from the learning one theorizes more accurately (Kronick, Cunningham & Gourley 2011 p. 32).

The interplay of theory and practice is a theme of Dewey's Dream (Benson, Harkavy, & Puckett 2007).

"There are ways in which the complex interrelationships between theory and practice transcend any effort at neat conceptualization. One of these is the application of service in our community and the use of community service as an academic research activity for students" (Benson et al. 2007 p. 55). It is a goal of the UACS to be transformative for both university students and at-risk children, their families, schools, and communities (Kronick, Dahlin-Brown, & Luter 2011).

The land-grant mission of universities was clearly explicated by the Morrill Act. This act established land-grant institutions that set in place one university in each state as its land-grant institution. Generally, agricultural education and military training were the backbone of this

74 *Robert F. Kronick*

act. It can be inferred that the Morrill Act was designed to get the university involved as a total entity, and civic engagement was a key feature of the university's culture. The following statement from Benson et al. exemplifies this stance. "The great universities of the 21st century will be judged by their ability to help solve our most urgent social problems" (p. 85). The other side of the coin is Urban Regime Theory where a handful of faculty do the important work (Shipps 1998). My experience is that Regime Theory is far more common than widespread involvement of the university. This widespread involvement is thoroughly discussed by Taylor & Luter (2013) in their work on anchor institutions, which they defined as institutions that did not move and were committed to working in the community where they are located. As a historical backdrop, the Morrill Act opened the doors of universities to non-elites. In other words, this act was rooted in supporting democracy in American society. In today's world, this is what Ira Harkavy and the Penn Group support. By offering access to non-elites, citizens could be educated about democratic values and ideals, and thus strengthen civic life in the nation. The state was recognizing for research and development to assist in the improvement of life conditions and economic development among the states, while opening its doors to the non-elite citizens of America (Alperowitz et al. 2008 p. 69).

The central thought is utility to do something for society which the existing colleges are not doing (Howard 1891 p. 336). At this time, a major objective of universities was to instill social responsibility and social contract to university students. This is quite a contrast with those who push jobs as the mean raison d'etre of colleges and universities.

As the role of agriculture changed, so did the impetus of the Morrill Act. Some universities have taken this transition in step by developing a more modern-day interpretation of the land-grant institution that includes service-learning centers, public policy experiences, and problem-based learning experiences and opportunities (Kronick et al. 2011). It is from this backdrop of the Morrill Act that engaged

Historical Antecedents 75

scholarship and scholar activism found at least a modicum of national and institutional support for the type of work done by university-assisted and other forms of community schools.

A conundrum here is will the work done by university students be ameliorative or transformative. The term service learning may even have questions of where is the service in service learning or where is the learning in service learning? Either way transformative, ameliorative, and the role of service and learning that play a pivotal role in service learning in engaged scholarship is a complex issue. These students working as service learners in community schools must comprehend that the community and the school are inseparable. As John Dewey so eloquently put in The School as Social Center. As current scholars, especially Henry Taylor, aver, where there are troubled communities, there are troubled schools (Taylor 1993). Benson et al. (2007 p. 55) maintain that the neighborhood is the prime community for children and youth who are educated in the school. They must have cohesive, organic communities that enable all community members to participate in the formation of the common will, feel that they are all members of a common wealth, and really have a share in society. This is truly Dewey's dream as articulated by the Penn Group, currently spearheaded by Ira Harkavy, long-time proponent of the university-assisted model of community schools.

SOME LOOKS AT SERVICE LEARNING

Kronick et al. offer the following as modes of understanding service learning:

- Service learning is serving while learning, acting to assist and benefit others while feeding one's own mind and heart.

- Service learning is open-ended, limited only by the creativity of someone who helps another and who in turn is enriched by what he/she has learned from the other (P.X1). This is reciprocity where both parties learn from the experience
- Service learning involves working with another and being introspective about what is happening in those moments of being in relationship with another (Kronick et al. p. X1). This is reflection. in doing service learning for twenty years on a university campus, I have found reflection the most difficult exercise for students to do. This may be due to the fact that they are rarely asked to take the time to think or feel about what they are doing. Csikszentmihalyi refers to this as a flow experience.
- Interaction of theory and practice is a critical component of service learning. It facilitates students' critical learning where students evaluate reading and classroom learning with what they learn in the field.

Reciprocity, reflection, and integration are the supports of study that is service learning.

EXPERIENTIAL LEARNING

Experiential learning has several iterations that are based on level of formality ranging from volunteering, to service learning, to internship and residency learning in medicine. These types of learning range from knowledge, comprehension, and application. Theoretical knowledge is generally most applicable in a classroom setting. Application is central to the work of scholar-activists. Most problems in living require applications/interventions that are based on sound, reified theory. The following vignette illustrates how theory developed in a situation where little knowledge and theory existed at the time.

Historical Antecedents 77

The setting is a Re-Ed school (Hobbs 1982) where the student was one with autism. At this time, our treatment team knew little about autism. The targeted behavior was one of self-stimulation where the child pulled skin off her arms. A punishment paired with a positive reinforcer was the intervention of choice. A punishment because the behavior had to be diminished or extinguished. The first punishment tried was alum, which was very abusive. The second was a water gun. It is this instance that is important to experiential learning and scholar activism. While using the water gun to stop the targeted behavior, a service learner alerted us to the almost certain possibility that the student would avoid water and stop drinking it. Without the assertion of the student, this deleterious intervention might well have continued indefinitely. The point of this vignette is that through service and experiential learning, the roles of teacher and student reverse, whereas the student knows more than the teacher about certain specific situations. I have found this to be so for many years.

ACTION THEORY

The interplay of action theory and service learning provides the answers to the question of where is the service in service learning and of course where is the learning.

Engaged scholarship and service learning are centerfolds for engaged universities and scholar activism. It is important to remember that the most important job of universities is the solving of social problems.

Action research is research that attempts to understand the world by changing it. Action theory emerges from action research. Experiential learning may be an example of action research. Action theory emerges from attempted social change. Action theory underlies the service-learning approach trying to make something better, and if it works, using the situation as evidence to support a theory compatible with the outcome (Argyris, Putnam, & Smith 1980, Kronick et al. 2011 p. 31).

With a few of the boys, a simple lunch room conversation can quickly escalate into a shooting match, and being their friend helps you get things under control more quickly (Kronick et al. 2011 p. 76).

This powerful quote illustrates how one learns from being out there. In this case, the one being out there is a student service learner rather than a faculty member. This illustrates that scholar activists are just as likely to be students as faculty. In fact, it is more likely that they are students. Faculty who do service learning must teach themselves to be experiential learners. The climate of engaged scholarship will facilitate this type of learning.

The following declaration is another example of learning by doing and carrying it forward:

> "Playing basketball with twenty-two children under the age of five and three other teachers, I heard shrieks tear across the gym. Like any instructor of young children, our eyes darted across the gym looking for the hurt child. I found the young man first. He was crying, but he did not have the words to say why. He seemed physically unharmed. His friend said he started crying after the gym became too loud. Myself being new to working with children, comforted him but remained puzzled about the seemingly unprovoked outburst" (W. Kronick 2018).

Four years earlier, Will Kronick learned from fellow staff (collaboration) that the outburst likely stemmed from the child's exposure to violence. Loud noises could have preceded physical harm at home. In hindsight, and now the practice of current programming, we prepare students for loud noises that will inevitably arise during play. Indeed, it remains impossible and undesirable to have silent play time, but instructors can coach children by teaching and modeling social and emotional learning.

W. H. Kronick, suicide prevention specialist, Tribal Family and Youth Services, Juneau, Alaska.

Historical Antecedents 79

Will's vignette is reminiscent of the child who started fights in school and was labelled as needing anger management, when in fact he was being assaulted in his home. Our response was to inform the man hitting him that he would go to jail if he did not stop. He did, and the little boy stopped fighting. So much for needs anger management.

TO GET STUCK INSIDE A MOBILE WITH THE MEMPHIS BLUES AGAIN – BOB DYLAN

In 2013 I had the extreme pleasure of teaching a service-learning course with a terrific group of students enrolled. One student, Feroza Freeland, a Memphian, stood out. Little did I know that Feroza would talk me into going to Memphis to explain our concept of University Assisted Community Schools. Memphis was in the midst of social change with white flight to trendy communities such as Germantown and Collierville. This left the city center essentially non-white. The non-white population was also poor. According to Marcus Pohlmann (2008), the most obvious difference between the city and county schools is race. Yet, following the desegregation efforts of the 1970s, the student body of the Memphis City Schools not only became noticeably blacker, but rather quickly also became noticeably poorer (p. 108). Pohlmann deduced that the main difference between the two groups city and county was their level of poverty. Jonathan Kozol, especially in *Savage Inequities*, has maintained that race explains more than socioeconomic status when it comes to educational outcomes such as grades, test scores, behavioral referrals, attendance, and tardies. I believe along with Pohlmann that poverty is the strongest predictor of school success. Two factors that have strongly influenced K-12 education is white flight to the suburbs and the formation of a school district for failing schools. This district has yielded little to no results and reliance on charter schools and vouchers. This combination of

80   *Robert F. Kronick*

charters and vouchers kept our community schools programs out of even the most basic elements. I will offer up my view that multiple providers of these private programs are making money from them. Here is a synopsis of what occurred on our trip to Memphis. I hope this will be helpful to those scholar activists who plan to bring about change, especially in K-12 public education. Poor children and families are political footballs.

- Who went to Memphis from Knoxville: an eclectic working team made up of graduate student Dareen Basma, undergraduate student Feroza Freeland, state representative Gloria Johnson, and UT professor Bob Kronick. The group shared strong support for community schools and a left-wing political stance. Freeland as a college sophomore spoke successfully before the state House against charters and vouchers. Today, she works for a legal entity promoting social justice in Tennessee. She has a chapter in a book edited by Kronick due out in late 2019. Her undergraduate thesis is on Memphis schools. She received a Chancellor's Award from the University of Tennessee in 2017. Dr. Basma is on the faculty and works in Carnegie Mellon's counseling center. She is also an adjunct faculty member at Paolo Alto University in California. She is co-author of a book with Kronick on University Assisted Community Schools. Her counseling skills came in handy as our meetings became heated more than once. Dr. Basma served as a counselor for members of the synagogue that was attacked in Pittsburgh. Representative Johnson was recently reelected and continues to promote community schools across the state and in the legislature. Kronick is proud to publish this book for Nova Science Publishers and advocate for community schools.

Historical Antecedents 81

OUTCOMES OF THE JOURNEY TO MEMPHIS

No progress was made in instituting community schools in Memphis/Shelby County Schools. The majority of failing schools in Tennessee are in Memphis city/Shelby County; however, our team was well-received by teachers and child care workers, and eighteen came to Knoxville to learn of University Assisted Community Schools and experience Pond Gap Elementary School, a UACS. It took this team a while to come to grips with the fact that Pond Gap is a public school. In late 2019, Pond Gap continues to thrive and vulnerable schools in Memphis continue to struggle. Their administration within the school system turns over, and the current governor supports outsourcing and supports charter schools and vouchers. He also has targeted rural schools but has made no promises. The UACS is beginning to work in a rural school. Some preliminary remarks follow at the end of this chapter. Needless to say, this was a failure experience which often leads to the rhetorical question of why would anyone not want a community school?

THIS IS THE END: THE DOORS

From Memphis to Morgan County, Tennessee. I end this chapter by opening the doors to our planning for a school in a rural area of East Tennessee with 594 residents and 400 children in a K-12 school. Over 50% of the children do not live with their birth parents. Many live with grandparents who ask for no financial help and are not able to help the children with homework. This will be a definite target for our UACS programs. The following are highlights to address in the near future and over time.

- Focus on assets, not exclusively deficits. The people, the rural environment, and a spirit of cooperation are assets.
- Report from meeting with governor. No promises were made. There is a commitment to rural areas across the county. The challenges are unique, including medical care or the lack thereof, opioid use, lack of opportunities post-high school, lack of technology across, and others yet to be determined. My work in this area is just beginning, but we are making collaborative commitments that we will keep. The resources of the university are at work here.
- Totally unexpected, I was invited to join a research group researching sustainable communities. This is in its beginning stages but hope springs eternal here.
- In the near future, our UACS program will offer Saturday science as a way of doing something concrete.

WHAT HAS HAPPENED AND WHAT WE MIGHT EXPECT IN THE FUTURE

"Moreover, civic engagement service learning, which were meant to be the vehicle used by the university to unleash its army of students, faculty, and staff to join with residents to solve problems and transform communities, never reached their potential. Instead of becoming engines of change, civic engagement service learning became mechanisms for teaching good citizenship, principles of liberal civic engagement, and do gooderism. The question is why?" (Taylor, Luter, & Uzochukwu 2018 p. 8). The starting point with this quest was the transformation of the United States into a people-centered cosmopolitan social democracy anchored by social and racial justice. The secret of this task according to the Penn Group is the racial transformation of three interactive socio-spatial sites: the university, the public school,

Historical Antecedents 83

and the under-developed neighborhood. The transformation of these three socio-spatial units will catalyze transformation of other dimensions of society (Taylor et al., 2018 p. 9).

Amelioration, transformation, and latte cities. What a great way to end this chapter. The issues are we cleaning up the water or fixing the leaks. Gentrification is an unanticipated consequence of transformative change. All done in the name of progress.

I wish you scholar activists well in this challenging and rewarding adventure. I wish you well.

Since October 4, 2010, a great deal of progress has occurred in our community schools. The following data outcomes were determined by Dr. R. Eric Heidel, director of research for the Graduate School of Medicine at the Knoxville campus of the University of Tennessee.

APPENDIX DATA

EVALUATION REPORT

University-Assisted Community Schools
Eric Heidel, PhD

INTRODUCTION

University-Assisted Community Schools (UACS) have the goal of positively impacting disparate populations of our nation's students. This external evaluation was conducted to test the effects of a UACS located at Pond Gap Elementary School in Knoxville, TN on standardized test scores related to math and reading. The time frame for this evaluation was from September to December of 2014. The second half of the evaluation will occur after the next administration of the tests.

METHODS

An observational retrospective cohort design was used to test the treatment effects of the UACS for first half of the school year. Eighty students that participated in UACS activities (treatment group) were compared to 160 matched students that did not participate in UACS activities (control group). These 160 control students were chosen using propensity score matching, with the variables of grade, gender, and ethnicity controlled for in a 2:1 control to case ratio matching scheme. There were several primary outcome variables chosen for analysis: Math scaled score, math grade equivalent, math curve equivalent, reading scaled score, reading grade equivalent, and reading curve equivalent. Kindergarten students were compared on a separate scaled score reading measure.

Mixed-effects ANOVAs were used to assess between-subjects (treatment vs. control) and within-subjects (preliminary test scores vs. post-intervention test scores). Skewness and kurtosis were used to confirm normality. Box's test of Equality and Mauchly's test of sphericity were employed to test for other statistical assumptions. Greenhouse-Geisser corrected p-values were interpreted as needed. All interactions were tested between gender, ethnicity, grade, and UACS participation. Statistical significance was assumed at a $p < .05$ level for each analysis and statistics were conducted using SPSS Version 21 (Armonk, NY: IBM Corp.).

RESULTS

Statistical assumptions for each analysis were met as per skewness, kurtosis, and Box's test. Greenhouse-Geisser corrected p-values were assessed accordingly. There was a significant increase in math scaled scores for all participants, regardless of UACS participation or not, *p* < .001. There was not a significant difference between UACS and non-UACS groups in terms of change in score over time, *p* = .66. However, UACS students scored higher on average at the post-intervention assessment (seven points higher).

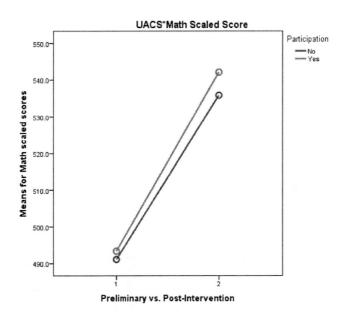

For math grade equivalent scores, there was a significant increase for all students in the study, p < .001. There was not a significant difference in how the UACS and non-UACS students changed across time, *p* = .64. UACS students did perform better than non-UACS students post-intervention.

For math curve equivalent scores, there was a significant increase for all participants, *p* < .001. There was not a significant difference between the UACS and non-UACS groups in how they changed across time, *p* = .49. However, the UACS students had a lower score at the preliminary observation and ended up performing higher than non-UACS students post-intervention. One can see this on the graph below because the "lines" cross.

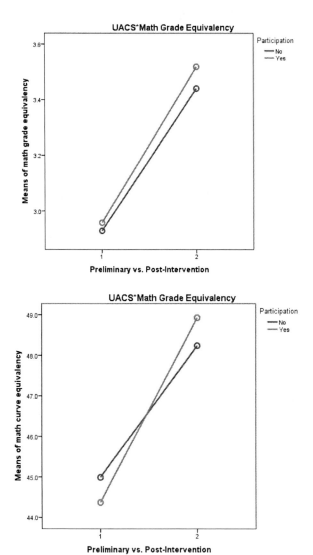

In regards to reading scaled scores, all students at Pond Gap, regardless of UACS participation, showed a significant increase, $p < .001$. There was not a difference between UACS and non-UACS participants changed across time, $p = .36$. UACS students performed higher than non-UACS students at both the preliminary and post-intervention observations.

Appendix Data

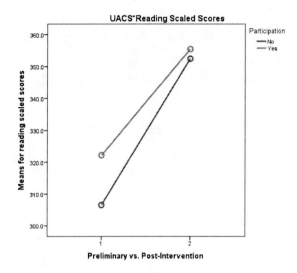

For reading grade equivalency scores, all students in the evaluation, regardless of UACS participated, had a significant increase from preliminary to post-intervention, $p < .001$. The groups did not differ in how they changed across time, $p = .39$. Again, UACS students performed better at both the preliminary and post-intervention observations.

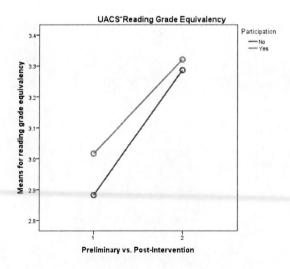

There was not a significant increase for all participants across time for reading curve equivalent, $p = .30$. There was also not a significant difference in how UACS groups changed across time, $p = .18$. UACS students performed higher at both observations as well.

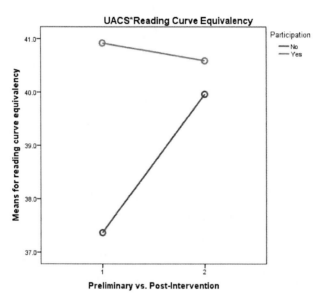

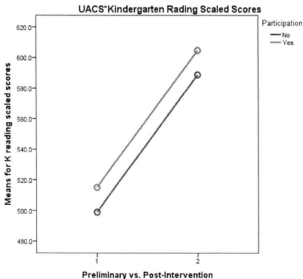

Appendix Data 91

The Kindergarten reading scaled score analysis found a significant increase for all students across time, $p < .001$. There was not a significant difference in how UACS and non-UACS students changed across time, $p = .99$.

INTERACTIONS

There was a significant interaction between UACS participation and gender for math scaled score, $p = .04$. Post hoc analysis showed that UACS boys (change from pre to post, 58.3 points) had a significantly higher change in math scaled score across time in comparison to non-UACS boys (change from pre to post, 36.8 points). A significant interaction was found with math grade equivalent score, UACS participation, and gender, $p = .02$. UACS boys (change from pre to post, 0.67) had a significantly higher rate of change than non-UACS boys (change from pre to post, 0.42). There was also a significant interaction between UACS participation and gender for math curve equivalent score, $p = .01$. UACS boys (change from pre to post, 6.1 points) experienced a significantly higher rate of change in math grade equivalent score than non-UACS boys (change from pre to post, 1.6 points).

There was a very interesting interaction between UACS participation, grade, ethnicity, and math grade equivalent score, $p = .009$. Post hoc analysis found that 2nd grade Hispanic UACS children (change from pre to post, 0.60 points) changed at a higher rate than 2nd grade Hispanic non-UACS children (change from pre to post, 0.17 points). UACS Caucasian children in the 2nd grade (change from pre to post, 1.0 points) changed at a higher rate than non-UACS Caucasian children in the 2nd grade (change from pre to post, 0.36 points). UACS Caucasian children in the 4th grade (change from pre to post, 0.83 points) changed at a higher rate than non-UACS Caucasian children in the 4th grade (change from pre to post, 0.43 points). Finally, UACS African American children in the 5th grade changed at a higher rate (change from pre to post, 1.1 points) than non-UACS African American children in the 5th grade (change from pre to post, 0.23 points) on math grade equivalency score.

DISCUSSION

The primary analysis found that a cohort of students at Pond Gap Elementary School, regardless of UACS participation, significantly increased on all outcome measures with the exception of reading curve equivalency scores, $p < .001$. This shows the laudable effort put forth by the teachers, administration, and staff at the school. Non-significant interactions were found between UACS participation and change across time for all outcome measures, $p > .05$. However, UACS students consistently scored higher on all outcome measures in comparison to non-UACS students.

Post hoc and sensitivity analyses found that certain subgroups gained more from the UACS program than others. UACS boys tended to have significantly higher increases in scores across time in comparison to non-UACS boys. Also, Caucasian, Hispanic, and African American children in the UACS program performed better than their counterparts in made grade equivalency scores.

This evaluation is only the first step in an objective and longitudinal evaluation project. Similar analyses will be run after the next test administration to detect any significant treatment effects and longitudinal implications of the UACS. While the "slope" or degree of change did not differ between UACS and non-UACS children, UACS participants scored higher on average on six out of seven outcome variables and underserved student populations experienced significant math grade equivalency score growth.

Appendix Data

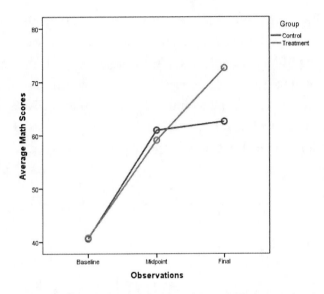

University Assisted Community School (UACS) students at Pond Gap Elementary School had significantly higher learning gains in Math across the 2017-2018 academic year in comparison to non-UACS students. Also, UACS at Pond Gap served over 10,000 dinners and after-school snacks to its students over the academic year.

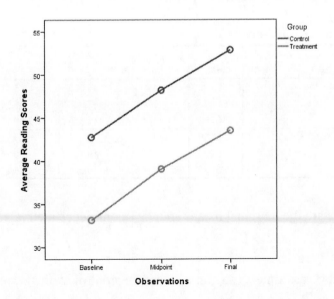

94   *Robert F. Kronick*

UACS students scored lower than non-UACS students across time on Reading scores for the 2017-2018 academic year. However, they had the same rate of increasing learning gains across time as the non-UACS students, which shows evidence of value-added learning gains associated with UACS interventions. Furthermore, UACS provided over 170 hours of tutoring and 170 hours of Arts Enrichment programming to over 100 students over the academic year.

Tests of Within-Subjects Effects

Measure: MEASURE_1

Source		Type III Sum of Squares	df	Mean Square	F	Sig.	Partial Eta Squared	Noncent. Parameter	Observed Power[a]
Read	Sphericity Assumed	416.345	2	208.173	4.372	.016	.114	8.744	.738
	Greenhouse-Geisser	416.345	1.858	224.135	4.372	.019	.114	8.121	.714
	Huynh-Feldt	416.345	2.000	208.173	4.372	.016	.114	8.744	.738
	Lower-bound	416.345	1.000	416.345	4.372	.044	.114	4.372	.529
Read * Group	Sphericity Assumed	688.901	2	344.450	7.234	.001	.175	14.468	.925
	Greenhouse-Geisser	688.901	1.858	370.862	7.234	.002	.175	13.438	.910
	Huynh-Feldt	688.901	2.000	344.450	7.234	.001	.175	14.468	.925
	Lower-bound	688.901	1.000	688.901	7.234	.011	.175	7.234	.743
Error(Read)	Sphericity Assumed	3237.858	68	47.616					
	Greenhouse-Geisser	3237.858	63.157	51.267					
	Huynh-Feldt	3237.858	68.000	47.616					
	Lower-bound	3237.858	34.000	95.231					

a. Computed using alpha = .05

There was a significant interaction between the treatment groups and reading in the 5th grade student, p = 0.002.

4. Group * Read

Measure: MEASURE_1

Group	Read	Mean	Std. Error	95% Confidence Interval	
				Lower Bound	Upper Bound
Control	1	55.750	5.248	45.085	66.415
	2	54.350	5.660	42.848	65.852
	3	54.300	5.874	42.363	66.237
Treatment	1	21.188	5.867	9.264	33.111
	2	26.000	6.328	13.141	38.859
	3	32.188	6.567	18.841	45.534

Here are the marginal means and 95% confidence intervals for these findings

And here is a graph showing the differences in how the groups changed across time. You can see that the control students were much

Appendix Data

higher in their scores for all three observations. However, look at how they essentially had a "plateau" across time...their scores did not change much across time. Now, look at the after-school students rate of change, it gradually increases across time. It is going up, while the control students have "plateaued." This is promising!

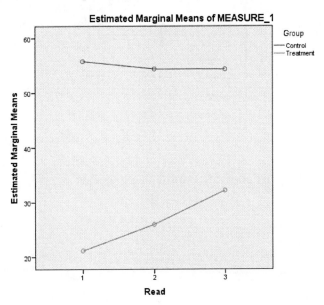

5th grade math scores

Tests of Within-Subjects Effects

Measure: MEASURE_1

Source		Type III Sum of Squares	df	Mean Square	F	Sig.	Partial Eta Squared	Noncent. Parameter	Observed Power[a]
Math	Sphericity Assumed	6545.744	2	3272.872	8.667	.000	.208	17.334	.963
	Greenhouse-Geisser	6545.744	1.870	3500.243	8.667	.001	.208	16.208	.954
	Huynh-Feldt	6545.744	2.000	3272.872	8.667	.000	.208	17.334	.963
	Lower-bound	6545.744	1.000	6545.744	8.667	.006	.208	8.667	.815
Math * Group	Sphericity Assumed	8151.573	2	4075.787	10.793	.000	.246	21.586	.988
	Greenhouse-Geisser	8151.573	1.870	4358.937	10.793	.000	.246	20.184	.983
	Huynh-Feldt	8151.573	2.000	4075.787	10.793	.000	.246	21.586	.988
	Lower-bound	8151.573	1.000	8151.573	10.793	.002	.246	10.793	.890
Error(Math)	Sphericity Assumed	24923.456	66	377.628					
	Greenhouse-Geisser	24923.456	61.713	403.862					
	Huynh-Feldt	24923.456	66.000	377.628					
	Lower-bound	24923.456	33.000	755.256					

a. Computed using alpha = .05

We have another significant interaction between the groups across time, p < 0.001.

4. Group * Math

Measure: MEASURE_1

Group	Math	Mean	Std. Error	95% Confidence Interval Lower Bound	95% Confidence Interval Upper Bound
Control	1	46.100	6.250	33.385	58.815
	2	52.950	6.005	40.732	65.168
	3	47.050	4.906	37.069	57.031
Treatment	1	44.533	7.216	29.852	59.215
	2	47.800	6.934	33.692	61.908
	3	81.333	5.665	69.808	92.858

Marginal means and 95% confidence intervals

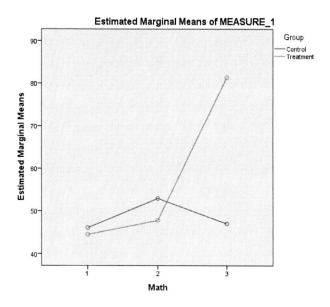

This is one to get excited about! Look at how the treatment group had such a large jump in math scores from observation 2 to observation 3! Wow!!!

Appendix Data

4th grade reading

Tests of Within-Subjects Effects

Measure: MEASURE_1

Source		Type III Sum of Squares	df	Mean Square	F	Sig.	Partial Eta Squared	Noncent. Parameter	Observed Power[a]
Read	Sphericity Assumed	12511.022	2	6255.511	41.256	.000	.596	82.513	1.000
	Greenhouse-Geisser	12511.022	1.231	10159.210	41.256	.000	.596	50.807	1.000
	Huynh-Feldt	12511.022	1.305	9583.707	41.256	.000	.596	53.858	1.000
	Lower-bound	12511.022	1.000	12511.022	41.256	.000	.596	41.256	1.000
Read * Group	Sphericity Assumed	15.289	2	7.644	.050	.951	.002	.101	.057
	Greenhouse-Geisser	15.289	1.231	12.415	.050	.871	.002	.062	.056
	Huynh-Feldt	15.289	1.305	11.712	.050	.883	.002	.066	.056
	Lower-bound	15.289	1.000	15.289	.050	.824	.002	.050	.055
Error(Read)	Sphericity Assumed	8491.022	56	151.625					
	Greenhouse-Geisser	8491.022	34.482	246.246					
	Huynh-Feldt	8491.022	36.553	232.296					
	Lower-bound	8491.022	28.000	303.251					

a. Computed using alpha = .05

Non-significant (NS) for reading between the groups, across time, p = 0.87.

4. Group * Read

Measure: MEASURE_1

Group	Read	Mean	Std. Error	95% Confidence Interval Lower Bound	Upper Bound
Control	1	32.667	7.090	18.144	47.190
	2	54.000	8.633	36.317	71.683
	3	59.933	8.575	42.368	77.499
Treatment	1	22.200	7.090	7.677	36.723
	2	45.133	8.633	27.450	62.817
	3	49.200	8.575	31.634	66.766

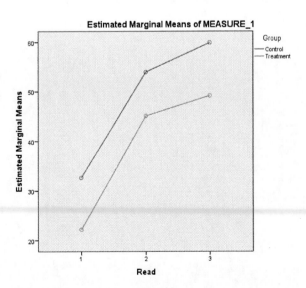

4th grade math

Tests of Within-Subjects Effects

Measure: MEASURE_1

Source		Type III Sum of Squares	df	Mean Square	F	Sig.	Partial Eta Squared	Noncent. Parameter	Observed Power[a]
Math	Sphericity Assumed	22728.745	2	11364.373	34.587	.000	.544	69.174	1.000
	Greenhouse-Geisser	22728.745	1.902	11948.768	34.587	.000	.544	65.791	1.000
	Huynh-Feldt	22728.745	2.000	11364.373	34.587	.000	.544	69.174	1.000
	Lower-bound	22728.745	1.000	22728.745	34.587	.000	.544	34.587	1.000
Math * Group	Sphericity Assumed	786.423	2	393.211	1.197	.310	.040	2.393	.252
	Greenhouse-Geisser	786.423	1.902	413.432	1.197	.308	.040	2.276	.246
	Huynh-Feldt	786.423	2.000	393.211	1.197	.310	.040	2.393	.252
	Lower-bound	786.423	1.000	786.423	1.197	.283	.040	1.197	.185
Error(Math)	Sphericity Assumed	19057.147	58	328.572					
	Greenhouse-Geisser	19057.147	55.163	345.468					
	Huynh-Feldt	19057.147	58.000	328.572					
	Lower-bound	19057.147	29.000	657.143					

a. Computed using alpha = .05

NS interaction, p = 0.31

4. Group * Math

Measure: MEASURE_1

Group	Math	Mean	Std. Error	95% Confidence Interval Lower Bound	Upper Bound
Control	1	30.875	6.939	16.684	45.066
	2	56.938	8.001	40.574	73.301
	3	63.125	7.124	48.556	77.694
Treatment	1	36.000	7.166	21.343	50.657
	2	59.533	8.263	42.634	76.433
	3	79.133	7.357	64.086	94.180

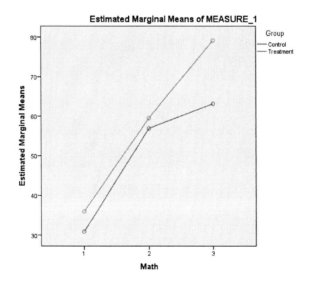

Appendix Data

This was not statistically significant, but look at the change in the treatment group from observation 2 to observation 3! It goes up, whereas for the control group, they start to stagnate in regards to growth in score from observation 2 to observation 3. Nice!

3rd grade reading

Tests of Within-Subjects Effects

Measure: MEASURE_1

Source		Type III Sum of Squares	df	Mean Square	F	Sig.	Partial Eta Squared	Noncent. Parameter	Observed Power[a]
Read	Sphericity Assumed	512.117	2	256.058	1.538	.221	.039	3.076	.317
	Greenhouse-Geisser	512.117	1.113	460.189	1.538	.224	.039	1.711	.238
	Huynh-Feldt	512.117	1.153	444.341	1.538	.224	.039	1.773	.242
	Lower-bound	512.117	1.000	512.117	1.538	.223	.039	1.538	.227
Read * Group	Sphericity Assumed	115.617	2	57.808	.347	.708	.009	.694	.104
	Greenhouse-Geisser	115.617	1.113	103.893	.347	.582	.009	.386	.091
	Huynh-Feldt	115.617	1.153	100.315	.347	.590	.009	.400	.091
	Lower-bound	115.617	1.000	115.617	.347	.559	.009	.347	.089
Error(Read)	Sphericity Assumed	12653.600	76	166.495					
	Greenhouse-Geisser	12653.600	42.288	299.225					
	Huynh-Feldt	12653.600	43.796	288.920					
	Lower-bound	12653.600	38.000	332.989					

a. Computed using alpha = .05

NS, p = 0.58

4. Group * Read

Measure: MEASURE_1

Group	Read	Mean	Std. Error	95% Confidence Interval Lower Bound	Upper Bound
Control	1	47.350	6.675	33.838	60.862
	2	49.600	6.693	36.050	63.150
	3	54.600	6.929	40.572	68.628
Treatment	1	45.750	6.675	32.238	59.262
	2	45.850	6.693	32.300	59.400
	3	48.200	6.929	34.172	62.228

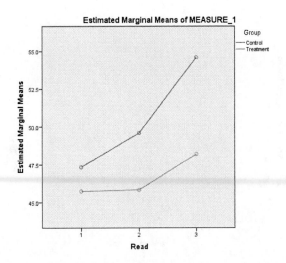

3rd grade math

Tests of Within-Subjects Effects

Measure: MEASURE_1

Source		Type III Sum of Squares	df	Mean Square	F	Sig.	Partial Eta Squared	Noncent. Parameter	Observed Power[a]
Math	Sphericity Assumed	21317.517	2	10658.758	46.598	.000	.551	93.195	1.000
	Greenhouse-Geisser	21317.517	1.867	11420.849	46.598	.000	.551	86.976	1.000
	Huynh-Feldt	21317.517	2.000	10658.758	46.598	.000	.551	93.195	1.000
	Lower-bound	21317.517	1.000	21317.517	46.598	.000	.551	46.598	1.000
Math * Group	Sphericity Assumed	724.850	2	362.425	1.584	.212	.040	3.169	.326
	Greenhouse-Geisser	724.850	1.867	388.338	1.584	.213	.040	2.957	.314
	Huynh-Feldt	724.850	2.000	362.425	1.584	.212	.040	3.169	.326
	Lower-bound	724.850	1.000	724.850	1.584	.216	.040	1.584	.233
Error(Math)	Sphericity Assumed	17384.300	76	228.741					
	Greenhouse-Geisser	17384.300	70.929	245.096					
	Huynh-Feldt	17384.300	76.000	228.741					
	Lower-bound	17384.300	38.000	457.482					

a. Computed using alpha = .05

NS, p = 0.21

4. Group * Math

Measure: MEASURE_1

Group	Math	Mean	Std. Error	95% Confidence Interval Lower Bound	Upper Bound
Control	1	39.750	4.834	29.965	49.535
	2	58.350	6.011	46.181	70.519
	3	65.750	6.190	53.219	78.281
Treatment	1	31.900	4.834	22.115	41.685
	2	60.800	6.011	48.631	72.969
	3	68.450	6.190	55.919	80.981

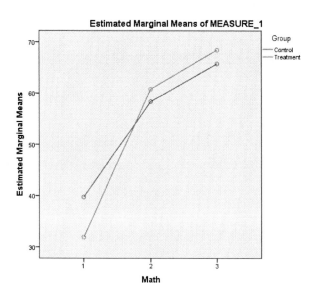

Appendix Data

2nd grade reading

Tests of Within-Subjects Effects

Measure: MEASURE_1

Source		Type III Sum of Squares	df	Mean Square	F	Sig.	Partial Eta Squared	Noncent. Parameter	Observed Power[a]
Read	Sphericity Assumed	2553.512	2	1276.756	11.367	.000	.331	22.734	.990
	Greenhouse-Geisser	2553.512	1.375	1856.956	11.367	.001	.331	15.631	.955
	Huynh-Feldt	2553.512	1.497	1705.479	11.367	.001	.331	17.019	.966
	Lower-bound	2553.512	1.000	2553.512	11.367	.003	.331	11.367	.898
Read * Group	Sphericity Assumed	209.192	2	104.596	.931	.401	.039	1.862	.201
	Greenhouse-Geisser	209.192	1.375	152.128	.931	.372	.039	1.281	.172
	Huynh-Feldt	209.192	1.497	139.719	.931	.379	.039	1.394	.178
	Lower-bound	209.192	1.000	209.192	.931	.345	.039	.931	.152
Error(Read)	Sphericity Assumed	5166.808	46	112.322					
	Greenhouse-Geisser	5166.808	31.627	163.365					
	Huynh-Feldt	5166.808	34.437	150.039					
	Lower-bound	5166.808	23.000	224.644					

a. Computed using alpha = .05

NS, p = 0.37

4. Group * Read

Measure: MEASURE_1

Group	Read	Mean	Std. Error	95% Confidence Interval Lower Bound	95% Confidence Interval Upper Bound
Control	1	39.923	8.792	21.735	58.111
	2	51.000	9.157	32.057	69.943
	3	58.154	8.444	40.685	75.623
Treatment	1	38.583	9.151	19.652	57.514
	2	44.083	9.531	24.367	63.800
	3	48.833	8.789	30.651	67.015

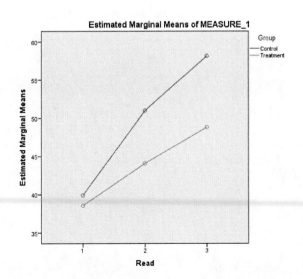

2nd grade math

Tests of Within-Subjects Effects

Measure: MEASURE_1

Source		Type III Sum of Squares	df	Mean Square	F	Sig.	Partial Eta Squared	Noncent. Parameter	Observed Power[a]
Math	Sphericity Assumed	25251.330	2	12625.665	29.773	.000	.564	59.546	1.000
	Greenhouse-Geisser	25251.330	1.875	13468.644	29.773	.000	.564	55.819	1.000
	Huynh-Feldt	25251.330	2.000	12625.665	29.773	.000	.564	59.546	1.000
	Lower-bound	25251.330	1.000	25251.330	29.773	.000	.564	29.773	.999
Math * Group	Sphericity Assumed	318.530	2	159.265	.376	.689	.016	.751	.107
	Greenhouse-Geisser	318.530	1.875	169.899	.376	.676	.016	.704	.105
	Huynh-Feldt	318.530	2.000	159.265	.376	.689	.016	.751	.107
	Lower-bound	318.530	1.000	318.530	.376	.546	.016	.376	.090
Error(Math)	Sphericity Assumed	19506.910	46	424.063					
	Greenhouse-Geisser	19506.910	43.121	452.377					
	Huynh-Feldt	19506.910	46.000	424.063					
	Lower-bound	19506.910	23.000	848.127					

a. Computed using alpha = .05

NS, p = 0.68

4. Group * Math

Measure: MEASURE_1

Group	Math	Mean	Std. Error	95% Confidence Interval Lower Bound	95% Confidence Interval Upper Bound
Control	1	39.923	7.647	24.104	55.742
	2	75.846	6.705	61.976	89.716
	3	84.308	5.493	72.945	95.670
Treatment	1	43.917	7.959	27.452	60.381
	2	82.000	6.979	67.564	96.436
	3	80.833	5.717	69.007	92.660

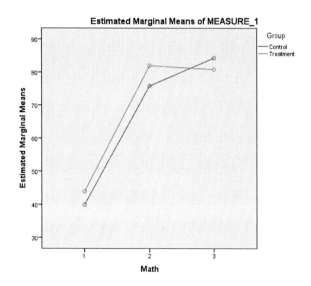

Appendix Data

1st grade reading

Tests of Within-Subjects Effects

Measure: MEASURE_1

Source		Type III Sum of Squares	df	Mean Square	F	Sig.	Partial Eta Squared	Noncent. Parameter	Observed Power[a]
Read	Sphericity Assumed	607.168	2	303.584	4.058	.023	.131	8.117	.698
	Greenhouse-Geisser	607.168	1.419	427.815	4.058	.038	.131	5.760	.590
	Huynh-Feldt	607.168	1.531	396.648	4.058	.034	.131	6.213	.613
	Lower-bound	607.168	1.000	607.168	4.058	.054	.131	4.058	.493
Read * Group	Sphericity Assumed	13.789	2	6.895	.092	.912	.003	.184	.063
	Greenhouse-Geisser	13.789	1.419	9.716	.092	.847	.003	.131	.062
	Huynh-Feldt	13.789	1.531	9.008	.092	.863	.003	.141	.062
	Lower-bound	13.789	1.000	13.789	.092	.764	.003	.092	.060
Error(Read)	Sphericity Assumed	4039.314	54	74.802					
	Greenhouse-Geisser	4039.314	38.319	105.412					
	Huynh-Feldt	4039.314	41.330	97.733					
	Lower-bound	4039.314	27.000	149.604					

a. Computed using alpha = .05

NS, p = 0.85

4. Group * Read

Measure: MEASURE_1

Group	Read	Mean	Std. Error	95% Confidence Interval Lower Bound	Upper Bound
Control	1	31.800	6.791	17.867	45.733
	2	30.000	7.139	15.351	44.649
	3	37.000	7.529	21.552	52.448
Treatment	1	35.857	7.029	21.435	50.280
	2	33.429	7.390	18.266	48.592
	3	39.143	7.793	23.152	55.133

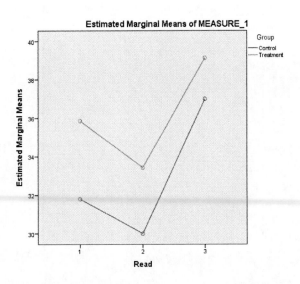

1st grade math

Tests of Within-Subjects Effects

Measure: MEASURE_1

Source		Type III Sum of Squares	df	Mean Square	F	Sig.	Partial Eta Squared	Noncent. Parameter	Observed Power[a]
Math	Sphericity Assumed	1901.400	2	950.700	2.904	.063	.094	5.807	.545
	Greenhouse-Geisser	1901.400	1.711	1111.346	2.904	.072	.094	4.968	.501
	Huynh-Feldt	1901.400	1.876	1013.362	2.904	.067	.094	5.448	.527
	Lower-bound	1901.400	1.000	1901.400	2.904	.099	.094	2.904	.377
Math * Group	Sphericity Assumed	1995.489	2	997.744	3.047	.055	.098	6.095	.567
	Greenhouse-Geisser	1995.489	1.711	1166.339	3.047	.064	.098	5.214	.521
	Huynh-Feldt	1995.489	1.876	1063.508	3.047	.059	.098	5.718	.548
	Lower-bound	1995.489	1.000	1995.489	3.047	.092	.098	3.047	.392
Error(Math)	Sphericity Assumed	18335.111	56	327.413					
	Greenhouse-Geisser	18335.111	47.905	382.738					
	Huynh-Feldt	18335.111	52.537	348.993					
	Lower-bound	18335.111	28.000	654.825					

a. Computed using alpha = .05

Very close to being significant, p = 0.06

4. Group * Math

Measure: MEASURE_1

Group	Math	Mean	Std. Error	95% Confidence Interval Lower Bound	95% Confidence Interval Upper Bound
Control	1	45.533	6.681	31.848	59.219
	2	66.667	7.222	51.873	81.461
	3	59.733	8.801	41.706	77.761
Treatment	1	51.200	6.681	37.514	64.886
	2	49.467	7.222	34.673	64.261
	3	56.600	8.801	38.572	74.628

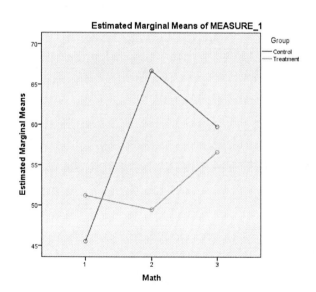

Appendix Data

Now, I aggregated all grades together into one large analysis.

Tests of Within-Subjects Effects

Measure: MEASURE_1

Source		Type III Sum of Squares	df	Mean Square	F	Sig.	Partial Eta Squared	Noncent. Parameter	Observed Power[a]
Read	Sphericity Assumed	8424.838	2	4212.419	31.128	.000	.165	62.256	1.000
	Greenhouse-Geisser	8424.838	1.556	5415.007	31.128	.000	.165	48.430	1.000
	Huynh-Feldt	8424.838	1.578	5337.548	31.128	.000	.165	49.133	1.000
	Lower-bound	8424.838	1.000	8424.838	31.128	.000	.165	31.128	1.000
Read * Group	Sphericity Assumed	3.888	2	1.944	.014	.986	.000	.029	.052
	Greenhouse-Geisser	3.888	1.556	2.499	.014	.967	.000	.022	.052
	Huynh-Feldt	3.888	1.578	2.463	.014	.969	.000	.023	.052
	Lower-bound	3.888	1.000	3.888	.014	.905	.000	.014	.052
Error(Read)	Sphericity Assumed	42762.649	316	135.325					
	Greenhouse-Geisser	42762.649	245.821	173.958					
	Huynh-Feldt	42762.649	249.389	171.470					
	Lower-bound	42762.649	158.000	270.650					

a. Computed using alpha = .05

NS for reading, p = 0.97

4. Group * Read

Measure: MEASURE_1

Group	Read	Mean	Std. Error	95% Confidence Interval Lower Bound	Upper Bound
Control	1	42.747	3.154	36.518	48.976
	2	48.217	3.316	41.668	54.766
	3	52.867	3.310	46.330	59.405
Treatment	1	33.143	3.274	26.676	39.610
	2	39.052	3.442	32.253	45.851
	3	43.519	3.437	36.732	50.307

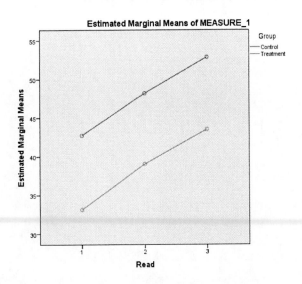

Aggregated math across all grades

Tests of Within-Subjects Effects

Measure: MEASURE_1

Source		Type III Sum of Squares	df	Mean Square	F	Sig.	Partial Eta Squared	Noncent. Parameter	Observed Power[a]
Math	Sphericity Assumed	61921.774	2	30960.987	80.290	.000	.336	160.579	1.000
	Greenhouse-Geisser	61921.774	1.947	31803.513	80.290	.000	.336	156.325	1.000
	Huynh-Feldt	61921.774	1.983	31223.041	80.290	.000	.336	159.231	1.000
	Lower-bound	61921.774	1.000	61921.774	80.290	.000	.336	80.290	1.000
Math * Group	Sphericity Assumed	3277.923	2	1638.961	4.250	.015	.026	8.501	.741
	Greenhouse-Geisser	3277.923	1.947	1683.567	4.250	.016	.026	8.275	.733
	Huynh-Feldt	3277.923	1.983	1652.839	4.250	.015	.026	8.429	.738
	Lower-bound	3277.923	1.000	3277.923	4.250	.041	.026	4.250	.536
Error(Math)	Sphericity Assumed	122625.630	318	385.615					
	Greenhouse-Geisser	122625.630	309.575	396.110					
	Huynh-Feldt	122625.630	315.330	388.880					
	Lower-bound	122625.630	159.000	771.230					

a. Computed using alpha = .05

There was a statistically significant interaction between the groups, across tie, $p = 0.016$.

4. Group * Math

Measure: MEASURE_1

Group	Math	Mean	Std. Error	95% Confidence Interval Lower Bound	95% Confidence Interval Upper Bound
Control	1	40.631	2.850	35.002	46.260
	2	60.988	3.132	54.802	67.174
	3	62.595	3.098	56.477	68.713
Treatment	1	40.792	2.977	34.913	46.671
	2	59.117	3.271	52.656	65.578
	3	72.662	3.236	66.272	79.053

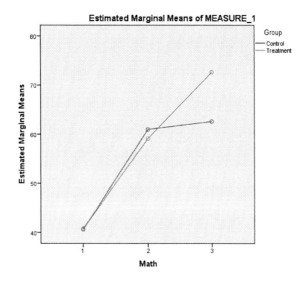

Appendix Data 107

WOW! Look at that change! Again, the rate of learning gains stays steady across time for the treatment group, whereas for the control group, it "plateaus." Nice!

7/1/2017 - 4/17/2018 7/1/2018 - 4/17/2019

Total School: 657 390

UACS 215 101

The rate of UACS referrals from 2017-2018 was 215/657 = 32.7%.

The rate of UACS referrals from 2018-2019 was 101/390 = 25.9%.

There was a statistically significant decrease in the rate of behavior referrals between the time periods, $X2(1) = 5.41$, $p = 0.02$.

Participants in the 2018/2019 group were 0.72 times less likely to have a behavior referral (95% CI 0.54 − 0.95) in comparison to the 2017-2018 group.

This first set of tables has the demographic information about the sample of students.

Grade					
		Frequency	Percent	Valid Percent	Cumulative Percent
Valid	K-1st grade	62	17.2	17.2	17.2
	2nd grade	57	15.8	15.8	33.0
	3rd grade	85	23.5	23.5	56.5
	4th grade	69	19.1	19.1	75.6
	5th grade	88	24.4	24.4	100.0
	Total	361	100.0	100.0	

Gender					
		Frequency	Percent	Valid Percent	Cumulative Percent
Valid	Male	201	55.7	55.7	55.7
	Female	160	44.3	44.3	100.0
	Total	361	100.0	100.0	

Robert F. Kronick

Status		Frequency	Percent	Valid Percent	Cumulative Percent
Valid	Part-time	80	22.2	43.2	43.2
	Full-time	105	29.1	56.8	100.0
	Total	185	51.2	100.0	
Missing	System	176	48.8		
Total		361	100.0		

Group		Frequency	Percent	Valid Percent	Cumulative Percent
Valid	Control	176	48.8	48.8	48.8
	Treatment	185	51.2	51.2	100.0
	Total	361	100.0	100.0	

Descriptive Statistics	N	Mean	Std. Deviation	Skewness		Kurtosis	
	Statistic	Statistic	Statistic	Statistic	Std. Error	Statistic	Std. Error
ELA 1	342	313.54	155.969	-.852	.132	-.232	.263
Math 1	349	241.47	146.807	.164	.131	-.919	.260
ELA 2	349	337.84	150.107	-.967	.131	.011	.260
Math 2	344	154.95	73.514	-.745	.131	-.108	.262
ELA 3	349	255.95	155.057	.151	.131	-.987	.260
Math 3	355	171.67	79.149	-.717	.129	-.171	.258
Absent	357	8.88	9.614	3.066	.129	13.879	.257
Behavior Referrals	355	.16	.943	9.255	.129	106.914	.258
Valid N (listwise)	313						

Here are the means and standard deviations for the observations of ELA, Math, Absences, and Behavioral Referrals. We are also testing the assumption of normality with skewness and kurtosis statistics. This assumption was violated for Absences and Behavioral Referrals, so, we will have to use non-parametric statistics for those comparisons.

It was readily evident to me when looking at the K-1st grade scores that they were different than the 2nd-5th grade scores. So, I am running analyses just for K-1st grade and then separate analyses for 2nd-5th grades.

K-1st ELA

Appendix Data

Tests of Within-Subjects Effects							
Measure: MEASURE_1							
Source		df	F	Sig.	Partial Eta Squared	Observed Powera
ELA	Sphericity Assumed	2	53.281	.000	.488	1.000
	Greenhouse-Geisser	1.894	53.281	.000	.488	1.000
	Huynh-Feldt	1.994	53.281	.000	.488	1.000
	Lower-bound	1.000	53.281	.000	.488	1.000
ELA * Group	Sphericity Assumed	2	48.155	.000	.462	1.000
	Greenhouse-Geisser	1.894	48.155	.000	.462	1.000
	Huynh-Feldt	1.994	48.155	.000	.462	1.000
	Lower-bound	1.000	48.155	.000	.462	1.000
Error(ELA)	Sphericity Assumed	112				
	Greenhouse-Geisser	106.075				
	Huynh-Feldt	111.640				
	Lower-bound	56.000				
a. Computed using alpha = .05							

There was a significant difference in the way that the treatment (UACS) and control (non-UACS) changed across time for ELA for K-1st grade students, $F(2,112) = 48.16$, $p < 0.001$, $\eta2 = 0.46$, power = 1.00.

4. Group * ELA					
Measure: MEASURE_1					
Group	ELA	Mean	Std. Error	95% Confidence Interval	
				Lower Bound	Upper Bound
Control	1	18.966	2.733	13.490	24.441
	2	63.448	5.798	51.833	75.064
	3	20.034	4.987	10.044	30.025
Treatment	1	14.966	2.733	9.490	20.441
	2	32.621	5.798	21.005	44.236
	3	48.310	4.987	38.320	58.301

Here are the marginal means and 95% confidence intervals for the two groups, across time.

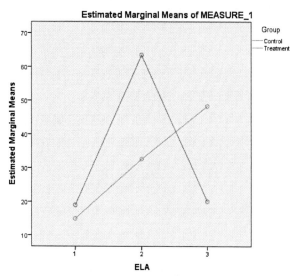

Here is a graphical depiction of the interaction. You can see that the control group went up and then back down. Whereas, the treatment group had a steady increase in scores across time.

K-1st Math

Tests of Within-Subjects Effects							
Measure: MEASURE_1							
Source		df	F	Sig.	Partial Eta Squared	Observed Power a
Math	Sphericity Assumed	2	12.261	.000	.177	.995
	Greenhouse-Geisser	1.826	12.261	.000	.177	.992
	Huynh-Feldt	1.917	12.261	.000	.177	.994
	Lower-bound	1.000	12.261	.001	.177	.931
Math * Group	Sphericity Assumed	2	33.507	.000	.370	1.000
	Greenhouse-Geisser	1.826	33.507	.000	.370	1.000
	Huynh-Feldt	1.917	33.507	.000	.370	1.000
	Lower-bound	1.000	33.507	.000	.370	1.000
Source		df	F	Sig.	Partial Eta Squared	Observed Power a
Error(Math)	Sphericity Assumed	114				
	Greenhouse-Geisser	104.100				
	Huynh-Feldt	109.253				
	Lower-bound	57.000				
a. Computed using alpha = .05							

Appendix Data

There was a significant difference in how the groups changed across time for the K-1st students, $F(2,114) = 33.51$, $p < 0.001$, $\eta 2 = 0.37$, power $= 1.00$.

4. Group * Math
Measure: MEASURE_1

Group	Math	Mean	Std. Error	95% Confidence Interval	
				Lower Bound	Upper Bound
Control	1	45.867	4.239	37.378	54.356
	2	19.800	3.456	12.880	26.720
	3	27.367	3.003	21.354	33.380
Treatment	1	13.034	4.312	4.400	21.669
	2	18.241	3.515	11.203	25.280
	3	23.241	3.054	17.126	29.357

Here are the marginal means and 95% confidence intervals for the interaction

You can see that the control group performed better than the treatment group at each time point. However, there was a steady increase across time for the treatment group. The slope of that change is similar to the ELA change (previous graph above).

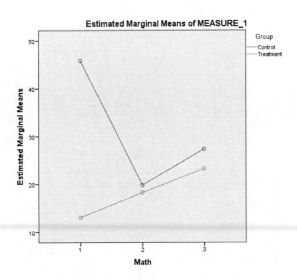

2nd-5th grade ELA

Tests of Within-Subjects Effects						
Measure: MEASURE_1						
Source		df	F	Sig.	Partial Eta Squared	Observed Powera
ELA	Sphericity Assumed	2	632.501	.000	.706	1.000
	Greenhouse-Geisser	1.832	632.501	.000	.706	1.000
	Huynh-Feldt	1.851	632.501	.000	.706	1.000
	Lower-bound	1.000	632.501	.000	.706	1.000
ELA * Group	Sphericity Assumed	2	946.637	.000	.782	1.000
	Greenhouse-Geisser	1.832	946.637	.000	.782	1.000
	Huynh-Feldt	1.851	946.637	.000	.782	1.000
	Lower-bound	1.000	946.637	.000	.782	1.000
Error(ELA)	Sphericity Assumed	528				
	Greenhouse-Geisser	483.596				
	Huynh-Feldt	488.650				
	Lower-bound	264.000				
a. Computed using alpha = .05						

There was a significant difference between the treatment and control groups in how they changed across time, $F(2,528) = 946.64$, $p < 0.001$, $\eta2 = 0.78$, power $= 1.00$.

4. Group * ELA					
Measure: MEASURE_1					
Group	ELA	Mean	Std. Error	95% Confidence Interval	
				Lower Bound	Upper Bound
Control	1	374.175	7.542	359.324	389.025
	2	395.167	6.790	381.797	408.536
	3	186.310	5.559	175.364	197.255
Treatment	1	381.414	7.155	367.326	395.503
	2	402.500	6.442	389.817	415.183
	3	413.936	5.274	403.552	424.320

Marginal means and 95% confidence intervals

Appendix Data

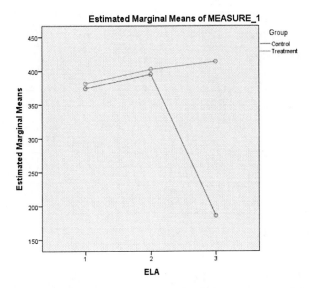

Here you can see that the treatment group performed better at all three time points and that there was a gradual increase across time, whereas the control group dropped off significantly between time point 2 and time point 3.

2nd-5th grade Math

Tests of Within-Subjects Effects							
Measure: MEASURE_1							
Source		df	F	Sig.	Partial Eta Squared	Observed Power[a]	
Math	Sphericity Assumed	2	1345.155	.000	.832	1.000	
	Greenhouse-Geisser	1.489	1345.155	.000	.832	1.000	
	Huynh-Feldt	1.501	1345.155	.000	.832	1.000	
	Lower-bound	1.000	1345.155	.000	.832	1.000	
Math * Group	Sphericity Assumed	2	1912.888	.000	.876	1.000	
	Greenhouse-Geisser	1.489	1912.888	.000	.876	1.000	
	Huynh-Feldt	1.501	1912.888	.000	.876	1.000	
	Lower-bound	1.000	1912.888	.000	.876	1.000	
Error(Math)	Sphericity Assumed	542					
	Greenhouse-Geisser	403.436					
	Huynh-Feldt	406.647					
	Lower-bound	271.000					
a. Computed using alpha = .05							

There was a significant difference between the groups in how they changed across time, $F(2,542) = 1912.89$, $p < 0.001$, $\eta 2 = 0.88$, power = 1.00.

4. Group * Math					
Measure: MEASURE_1					
Group	Math	Mean	Std. Error	95% Confidence Interval	
				Lower Bound	Upper Bound
Control	1	389.231	5.466	378.470	399.992
	2	173.277	3.554	166.281	180.273
	3	197.046	3.994	189.183	204.909
Treatment	1	181.951	5.212	171.691	192.211
	2	194.727	3.388	188.056	201.398
	3	207.811	3.808	200.314	215.308

Marginal means and 95% confidence intervals

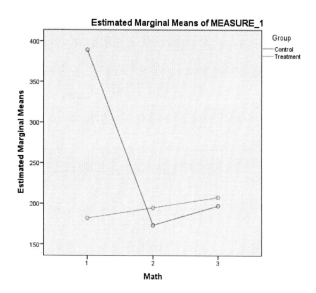

Here again, you can see a steep dropoff for the control group, whereas the treatment group had a steady increase across time.

Comparison of groups on absences and behavioral referrals, 2nd-5th grade

Appendix Data 115

Test Statisticsa	Absent	Behavior Referrals
Mann-Whitney U	8068.500	10215.000
Wilcoxon W	19696.500	21843.000
Z	-3.916	-1.661
Asymp. Sig. (2-tailed)	.000	.097
a. Grouping Variable: Group		

There was a significant difference between the UACS and non-UACS groups for absences, p < 0.001. There was a non-significant difference for behavior referrals, p = 0.10.

Descriptives	Group		Statistic
Absent	Control	Median	7.00
		Interquartile Range	11
	Treatment	Median	5.00
		Interquartile Range	7
Behavior Referrals	Control	Median	.00
		Interquartile Range	0
	Treatment	Median	.00
		Interquartile Range	0

Here are the medians and interquartile ranges for the groups. For absences, the control group was significantly higher (median = 7.0, IQR = 11.0) than the treatment group (median = 5.0, IQR = 7.0).

Same comparison, K-1st grade

Test Statisticsa	Absent	Behavior Referrals
Mann-Whitney U	322.000	448.000
Wilcoxon W	850.000	976.000
Z	-2.055	-1.473
Asymp. Sig. (2-tailed)	.040	.141
a. Grouping Variable: Group		

There was a significant difference between the groups for absences, p = 0.04, but not for behavioral referrals, p = 0.14.

Descriptivesa			Statistic
	Group		
Absent	Control	Median	8.00
		Interquartile Range	12
	Treatment	Median	5.00
		Interquartile Range	6
Behavior Referrals	Control	Median	.00
		Interquartile Range	0
a. Behavior Referrals is constant when Group = Treatment. It has been omitted.			

The number of absences was significantly higher in the control group (median = 8.00, IQR = 12.00) versus the treatment group (median = 5.00, IQR = 6.00).

There were no behavioral referrals in the treatment group.

EPILOGUE

This tidy little book is packed full of exciting, different, and hopefully helpful materials for those aspiring scholar activists who want to do their work in the community and who also want to see their universities engaged in this work. As culture shifts once again or continually bombards campuses with big science, the guts of the university, the humanities and social sciences may yet again suffer blasts from government in the manner of funding. On my campus, science, engineering, and high-speed computers all are receiving generous support including new buildings. U.S. Senator Lamar Alexander has provided ample support for these programs from his pulpit. I have not seen much for humanities, social sciences, and the helping fields. I do not begrudge these fields their largesse, but I know there is more to large research I universities than big science. To all who read this book, I hope you will work to get your universities engaged in your communities. Community schools need your attention and support, and I firmly believe they are superior to charter schools and vouchers who put money into the hands of private sector bureaucrats who don't even get the basic importance of working with and cooperating with local school people much less collaborating with them is astounding. Memphis and New Orleans are examples of charters and vouchers running amok. Even the flamboyant Geoffrey Canada has been silent on the successes of the Harlem Children's Zone.

REFERENCES

Agee, J. & Evans, W. (1940). *Let Us Now Praise Famous Men*. Boston: Houghton Mifflin.

Alexander, M. (2012). *The New Jim Crow: Mass Incarceration in the Age of Colorblindness*. The New Press. New York, NY.

Alperowitz, G., S. Dubb, & T. Howard. (2008). The Next Wave: Building University Engagement. *21st Century Press Journal*. 7(2). 69-75.

Argyris, C., Putnam, R., & D. Smith. (1985). *Action Science*. Jossey-Bass. San Francisco, CA.

Behrstock, B. (2007). *The Way of the Artist: Reflections on Creativity and the Life, Home, Art and Collections of Richard Marquis*. California State University. Fullerton, CA.

Benson, L., I. Harkavy, & J. Puckett. (2007). *Dewey's Dream*. Temple University Press. Philadelpia, PA.

Bronfrenbrenner, U. (1979). *The Ecology of Human Development*. Harvard University Press. Cambridge, MA.

Coles, R. (1993). *The Call of Service. A Witness to Idealism*. Houghton Mifflin. Boston, MA.

Comer, J. (1996). *Rallying the Whole Village*. Teachers' College Press. New York, NY.

120 *References*

Csikszentmihalyi, M. (1970). University of Chicago Press. Chicago, IL.

Desmond, M. (2016). *Evicted: Poverty and Profit in the American City.* Crown Publishers. New York, NY.

Dryfoos, J. (1994). *Full-Service Schools: A Revolution in Health and Social Services for Children, Youth, and Families.* Jossey-Bass. San Francisco, CA.

Ehrenerich, B. (2001). *Nickel and Dimed.* New York. Henry Holt.

Eisner, E. (1998). *The Kinds of Schools Our Kids Need.* Heineman. Portsmouth, NH.

Ferrara, J. & Jacobson, R. (2019). *Community Schools: People and Races Transforming Education and Communities.* Rowman & Littlefield. New York, New York.

Forman Jr., J. (2017). *Locking Up Our Own: Crime and Punishment in Black America.* Farrar, Strauss, and Giroux. New York.

Friedrich, D. (1975). *Going Crazy.* New York: Simon & Shuster.

Gladwell, M. (2014). The Crooked Ladder: The Criminals Guide to Upward Mobility. *Urban Chronicles.* New York, NY.

Goffman, A. (2014). *On the Run: Fugitive Life in an American City.* University of Chicago Press. Chicago, IL.

Goffman, E. (1963). *Stigma: Notes on the Management of Spoiled Identity.* Prentice Hall. Englewood Cliffs, NJ.

Guy, R. (2019). *Will the Real Hillbilly Please Stand Up? Urban Appalachian Migration and Culture Seen Through the Lens of Hillbilly Elegy.* p. 86-104 in Appalachian Reckoning. A. Harkins & M. McCarroll eds.

Harkavy, I. & B. Donovan. (2005). *Connecting Past and Present: Concepts and Models for Service-learning in History.* American Association for Higher Education. Washington, DC.

Harkins A. & M. McCarroll eds. (2019). *Appalachian Reckoning: A Region Responds to Hillbilly Elegy.* West Virginia University Press. Charleston, WV.

Hobbs, N. (1982). *The Troubled and the Troubling Child.* Jossey-Bass. San Francisco, CA.

References 121

Holley, K. & Colyar, J. (2009). Rethinking Texts: Narrative & the Construction of Qualitative Research. *Educational Researcher*. Vo. 38 #9 680-686.

Jones, T. (2019). *Toni Morrison Time Magazine* pp. 42-44. New York, NY. August 19, 2019.

Kronick, B. & D. Basma. (2017). *Wicked Problems and the Community School Solution.* Nova Science Publishers. New York, NY.

Kronick, R. (2000). *Human Services and the Full-Service School.* Charles C. Thomas Press. Springfield, IL.

Kronick, R. (2002). *Full-Service Schools. Encyclopedia of Education.* McMillan. New York, NY.

Kronick, R. (2005). *Full Service Community Schools: Prevention of Delinquency in Students with Mental Illness.* Charles C. Thomas Publishers. Springfield, IL.

Kronick, R. (2006). Probation and Headlice: The Intersection of Corrections and Education. *The Educational Forum.* 70(2). 104-115.

Kronick, R. & D. Thomas. (2008). Carl Upchurch: Prisoner Citizen. Labeling Theory and Symbolic Interaction. *Journal of Progressing Human Services.* 19(2). 112-124.

Kronick, R. & R. Cunningham. (2013). Service Learning: Some Academic and Community Recommendations. *Journal of Higher Education Outreach and Engagement.* 17(3). 121-134.

Kronick, R., N. Dahlin-Brown, & D. G. Luter. (2011). Revitalizing the Land Grant Mission in the South: One University's Path to Civic Engagement Via Community Schools pp. 203-217. In *Exploring Cultural Dynamics and Tensions within Service Learning.* Hobbs, N. (2011). Information Age Publishing. Charlotte, NC.

Kronick, R., R. Cunningham, & Gourley. (2011). *Experiencing Service Learning.* University of Tennessee Press. Knoxville, TN.

Kronick, W. H. (2018). Unpublished Document.

Lee, B. (2010). In *Consideration of Photographing in the South.*

References

Lemert, E. (1967). *Human Deviance, Social Problems, and Social Control*. Prentice Hall. Englewood Cliffs, NJ.

Lester, J., R. Kronick, & M. Benson. (2012). *A University Joins the Community*. Phi Delta Kappan. 93 (6). 42-45.

Lewis, O. (1952). *Review of Life in a Mexican Village*: Tepoztlan Restudied. University of Illinois Press.

Maier, A., J. Daniel, J. Oakes, & L. Lam. (2017). *Community Schools as an Effective School Improvement Strategy*. Learning Policy Institute. Palo Alto, CA. A Review of the R. Kronick and C. Hargis (1998). Dealing with Dropouts. 2nd ed. Charles C. Thomas. Springfield, IL.

Martinson, R. (1974). *What Works? Questions and Answers About Prison Reform*. The Public Interest. 22-34.

Maslow, A. (1943). A Theory of Human Motivation. *Psychological Review*. 50(4). 370-396. Washington, DC.

Moffatt, F. (2009). *The Life, Art, & Times of Joseph Delaney*. Knoxville: University of Tennessee Press.

Nash, R. (2004). *Liberating Scholarly Writing: The Power of Personal Narrative*. New York: Teachers College Press.

Nisbet, R. (1976). *Sociology as an Art Form*. New York: Oxford University Press.

Noguera, P. (2011). A broader and bolder approach uses education to break the cycle of poverty: making bold assertions that all children can achieve while doing nothing to address the challenges they face is neither fair nor sound public policy. *Phi Delta Kappan*. 93(3) pp. 8-14. retrieved from http://journals.sagepub.com/doi/2011/10.1177. 003172171109300303.

O'Connor, A. (2001). *Poverty Knowledge Social Science, Social Policy and the Poor in Twentieth Century* O.C. History. Princeton: Princeton University Press.

Oakes, J., A. Maier, & J. Daniel. (2017). *Community Schools: An Evidence-Based Strategy for Equitable School Improvement*.

References 123

Education Policy Center. Boulder, CO. Retrieved from https://Eric.ed.gov/?id=ed-574713.

Parsons, T. (1959). *The School as a Social System. Some of its Functions in American Society.* Harvard University Press. 29(4). 297-313.

Polhmann, M. (2008). *Opportunity Lost: Race and Poverty in the Memphis City Schools.* University of Tennessee Press. Knoxville, TN.

Ryan, W. (1971). *Blaming the Victim. Random House.* New York, NY.

Schur, E. (1965). *Crimes Without Victims.* Prentice Hall. Englewood Cliffs, NJ.

Taylor, H. (1993). *Race and the City: Work, Community, and Protest in Cincinnati 1820-1970.* University of Illinois Press. Champaign, IL.

Taylor, H., D. G. Luter, & K. Uzochukwo. (2018). The Truthful Mirror: Reforming the Civic Engagement Movement in Higher Education. In Kronick R. F. (ed.), *Community Engagement: Principles, Strategies, and Practices.* Nova Science Publishers. New York, New York.

Upchurch, C. (1996). Convicted in the Womb: One Man's Journey from Prisoner to Peacemaker. *Bantam Books.* New York, NY

Whitehead, C. (2019). *Nickel Boys.* Doubleday. New York, NY.

Winn, M. & N. Behizadeh, (2011). The Right to be Literate: Literacy, Education, and the School-to-Prison Pipeline. *Review of Research in Education.* 35(1). 147-173.

Wofford, J. (1970). *Urban Universities: Rhetoric, Reality, and Conflict.* U.S. Department of Health, Education, and Welfare.

AUTHOR'S CONTACT INFORMATION

Dr. Robert Kronick
Professor Emeritus
University of Tennessee, Knoxville, Tennessee
Email: rkronick@utk.edu

INDEX

A

academic learning, 58
academic performance, 59
academic progress, 10
academic success, 11, 58, 59
access, 31, 74
action research, 77
Action Theory, 77
activism, 4, 75, 77
adjustment, 30
administrators, 71
adult education, 69
adults, 4
advancement, 2
advocacy, 69
aesthetic, 29
African Americans, 49
age, 27, 29, 61, 78
Agee, James, 3, 7, 16, 17, 19, 20, 21, 22, 23, 24, 25, 26, 27, 28, 29, 30, 31, 32, 33, 34, 43, 51, 119
agencies, 11, 41
agency collaboration, 36
agriculture, 74
alcoholics, 2
American Educational Research Association, 53

anger, 4, 26, 45, 48, 64, 79
anxiety, 11
arrests, 3
assessment, 66, 87
assets, 10, 71, 82
asthma, 5
attachment, 16
autism, 77

B

Baldwin, James, 46, 47
barriers, 1, 35
basic needs, 58
behaviors, 6, 46, 50, 51
benefits, 45, 59
birds, 39
blame, 35
blood, 10
Boone, North Carolina, 55
boredom, 21, 30
bottom-up, 12
brain, 30
brain tumor, 30
breastfeeding, 29
brothers, 46

128 *Index*

C

caricature, 16
challenges, 35, 82, 122
Chicago, 18, 120
childcare, 41
children, 6, 8, 9, 11, 12, 13, 14, 16, 17, 29,
    30, 31, 35, 36, 37, 38, 39, 40, 41, 47, 49,
    56, 59, 62, 64, 69, 73, 75, 78, 80, 81, 91,
    92, 122
circus, 57, 62
cities, 13, 83
citizens, 46, 74
citizenship, 82
civic life, 74
civil rights, 13
civil society, 37
classes, 60, 61, 62, 63, 69
classroom, 55, 67, 76
cleaning, 83
climate, 78
Clinic Vols, 36
clothing, 25, 29, 30, 32, 35, 48
Coalition of Community Schools, 53
cognitive abilities, 61
coherence, 7, 22
coke, 29
Coles, Robert, 30, 49
collaboration, 10, 11, 34, 36, 40, 78
collaborative approaches, 37
colleges, 67, 74
color, 5, 47, 48
communication, 62, 69
communities, 9, 13, 15, 16, 18, 36, 39, 41,
    44, 52, 70, 73, 75, 79, 82, 117
community, 6, 8, 9, 11, 12, 13, 14, 15, 16,
    19, 20, 34, 35, 36, 37, 38, 39, 40, 41, 42,
    50, 52, 53, 54, 55, 56, 57, 58, 59, 62, 70,
    71, 73, 74, 75, 80, 81, 83, 117
community involvement, 11, 70
community service, 73

compassion, 62
complexity, 3, 7
complications, 24
comprehension, 76
conceptualization, 73
conference, 37
confidence, 61, 63, 94, 96, 109, 111, 112,
    114
conflict, 49
consciousness, 33
consensus, 9, 30, 36, 53
construction, 10, 23, 63
control group, 86, 99, 107, 110, 111, 112,
    113, 114, 115, 116
conversations, 28, 31
Convicted in the Womb, 39, 45, 47, 123
cooking, 41, 57, 63
cooperation, 82
correlation, 5, 30, 47
counseling, 10, 36, 80
creativity, 29, 30, 76
credentials, 41, 69
criminal behavior, 3, 17
criminal justice system, 6, 45
cultural differences, 40
culture, 6, 9, 15, 16, 20, 24, 49, 56, 60, 61,
    71, 74, 117
cure, 20
cures, 24
curriculum, 9, 10, 14, 57, 60, 62

D

Davis, Blenza, 3, 54
defendants, 3, 38
deficit, 5, 10
delinquency, 46, 50
delinquent acts, 57
democracy, 74, 82
disappointment, 45, 47
discrimination, 5

Index   129

disorder, 31
distress, 45, 48
distribution, 63
donations, 65
donors, 62
Dow Chemical, 54, 55
Dozier School, 44, 45
dream, 2, 75
drug offense, 38
Dryfoos, Joy, 16, 36, 42, 53, 54

E

ecology, 6, 35
economic development, 74
economic status, 29
education, 2, 12, 13, 26, 30, 38, 56, 61, 62,
    63, 66, 73, 79, 122
educational programs, 62, 70
educational research, 49
educational system, 26
elementary school, 49
emotional intelligence, 62
empathy, 21, 41
employees, 12, 57, 70
Encyclopedia of Education, 38, 121
engineering, 41, 63, 117
environment, 2, 4, 18, 20, 30, 31, 41, 57, 59,
    61, 62, 69, 82
environments, 10, 31
equipment, 25
equity, 38
erosion, 8, 28
ethnicity, 86, 91
Evans, Walker, 7, 16, 17, 20, 21, 22, 24, 25,
    26, 27, 28, 31, 32, 33, 34, 43, 51, 119
evidence, 78, 94
exercise, 76
expertise, 13, 57
exposure, 61, 78

F

families, 5, 6, 9, 11, 12, 16, 20, 24, 25, 26,
    31, 32, 36, 37, 38, 39, 41, 42, 44, 53, 59,
    63, 69, 73, 80
family members, 5
feelings, 27, 53
fights, 4, 79
financial, 36, 81
fitness, 61, 62
flight, 44, 79
flow, 76
food, 12, 35, 48, 62, 63
football, 48
formation, 75, 79
fraud, 44
free world, 45
frostbite, 17
functional analysis, 1
funding, 42, 64, 65, 117
funds, 38, 64

G

germination, 53
gifted, 38
governor, 81, 82
grades, 30, 31, 41, 59, 66, 79, 105, 106, 108
graduate students, 36
growth, 59, 65, 92, 99

H

Hale County, Alabama, 17, 20, 24, 26, 30,
    32, 44
healing, 56
health, 9, 11, 22, 30, 36, 57, 58, 61, 62, 63,
    69
health care, 36, 57
health services, 58

130   *Index*

high school, 11, 48, 49, 82
higher education, 15
history, 14, 49, 60
Holst, Karen, 57, 58
homelessness, 39
homes, 5, 15, 25
homework, 59, 66, 67, 69, 81
housing, 5, 35, 40, 41, 46, 47
hub, 9, 16, 40, 62
human, 3, 4, 5, 6, 7, 9, 23, 26, 28, 33, 41, 43, 44, 48, 51, 56
human behavior, 3, 7, 23, 33, 48, 51
human condition, 28, 33, 43, 44
human development, 6
human perception, 26

I

ideals, 74
identification, 16
identity, 48, 50
If Beale Street Could Talk, 46
illusion, 51
image, 15, 23
images, 23
imprisonment, 47
impulsiveness, 64
individuality, 21
individuals, 5, 18, 29, 31, 46
institutions, viii, 2, 15, 45, 52, 73
interdependence, 59
intermediaries, 40
internship, 76
interpersonal skills, 59
intervention, 52, 64, 68, 77, 86, 87, 88, 89
intimacy, 27
investments, 39
IQR, 115, 116
isolation, 50
issues, 9, 11, 15, 24, 27, 36, 40, 47, 48, 50, 63, 68, 83

J

journalists, 24
just society, 16
juveniles, 39

K

kindergarten, 11

L

labeling, 31
lack of opportunities, vii, 82
landscape, 28
Lane, Stonney Ray, 56
languages, 61
latte cities, 83
lawyers, 38
lead, 13, 14, 22, 52, 60
leadership, 10, 37, 65
leaks, 83
learners, 20, 75, 78
learning, 11, 13, 15, 20, 30, 35, 36, 38, 51, 57, 58, 59, 61, 62, 66, 67, 70, 73, 74, 75, 76, 77, 78, 79, 82, 93, 94, 107, 120
learning environment, 58
Lee, Baldwin, 4, 7, 8, 19, 20, 25, 27, 28, 36, 51
light, ix, 24, 51
love, 11, 32, 51, 52, 56

M

Malcolm X, 47
management, 4, 64, 79
materials, 60, 69, 117
mathematics, 65, 66
measurement, 52
media, 46

Index   131

median, 115, 116
medical, 37, 82
medical care, 82
medicine, 13, 36, 76
mental health, 9, 30, 35, 36, 41, 47, 54, 56, 58, 63, 68
mental illness, 30, 31, 46
mentoring, 64, 70
mentoring program, 64
migrants, 16
military, 73
mission, 28, 73
modus operandi, 44
Morrill Act, 73, 74
Morrison, Toni, 47, 121
motivation, 24
music, 7, 11, 16, 22, 57, 59, 60

N

negativity, 48
Nickel Boys, 43, 45, 46, 48, 52, 123
Noguera, Pedro, 12, 122
nursing, 13, 36
nutrition, 60, 61, 63

O

offenders, 39
officials, 52
oil, 30
opportunities, 11, 35, 36, 38, 58, 69, 74
optimism, 55
outsourcing, 81
ownership, xi, 63

P

paradigm shift, 13
parent involvement, 11

parents, 9, 11, 14, 29, 36, 40, 45, 62, 64, 68, 69, 81
parole, 4, 46
participants, 51, 86, 87, 88, 90, 92
peace, 56
Penn Group, 41, 42, 54, 74, 75, 82
performance goals, 67
personal goals, 48
personal life, 7, 8, 70
personality, 6
Philadelphia, 3, 39, 45, 54
photographers, 26
photographs, 25, 27, 34
physical activity, 58, 61
physical education, 59, 62
physical fitness, 60, 61, 63
pleasure, 27, 79
police, 25, 50
policy, 5, 41, 69
population, 39, 40, 79
poverty, 3, 6, 9, 11, 13, 19, 23, 24, 32, 33, 38, 47, 55, 58, 79, 122
preparation, iv, 63
prevention, 10, 36, 54, 78
principles, 21, 40, 82
problem children, 31
problem solving, 66, 68
problem-based learning, 74
professional development, 67, 68, 70
professionals, 10
program staff, 69
programming, 40, 59, 60, 62, 63, 67, 70, 78, 94
project, 19, 25, 31, 34, 58, 66, 70, 92
psychiatrist, 14
psychology, 13, 36, 55
public education, 49, 80
public health, 13
public policy, 74, 122
public schools, 12, 49
publishing, 43
punishment, 77

132 *Index*

R

race, 20, 45, 47, 61, 79
rate of change, 91, 95
Ray, James Earl, 56
reading, vii, 5, 48, 57, 59, 60, 61, 65, 66, 76, 85, 86, 88, 89, 90, 91, 92, 94, 97, 99, 101, 103, 105
reality, 23, 24, 51
recreation, 13
Re-Ed, 77
reforms, 35
Regime Theory, 74
reinforcement, 50
rejection, 2, 45, 47
reputation, 52
requirement, 48
researchers, 7, 26, 52
resources, 13, 38, 41, 69, 82
response, 8, 12, 36, 48, 79
rural poverty, 32
rural school, 71, 81
rural schools, 81

S

safety, 56
Sample, Blaine, 41, 57, 58
scholarship, 15, 17, 37, 62, 75, 77, 78
school, 2, 3, 4, 6, 7, 8, 9, 10, 11, 12, 13, 14, 15, 16, 20, 21, 23, 30, 31, 35, 36, 37, 38, 39, 40, 41, 42, 43, 45, 47, 48, 49, 50, 52, 53, 54, 55, 57, 58, 59, 60, 61, 62, 63, 64, 65, 67, 68, 69, 71, 73, 75, 77, 79, 80, 81, 82, 83, 86, 92, 93, 95, 117
school activities, 58
school culture, 49
school failure, 14
school learning, 58
school performance, 12
school psychology, 36

school success, 9, 79
science, 7, 11, 18, 19, 20, 21, 23, 24, 31, 44, 51, 57, 63, 66, 71, 82, 117
secondary deviance, 50
self-concept, 30
self-discipline, 62
self-esteem, 60, 64
self-improvement, 62
service learning, 13, 15, 70, 75, 76, 77, 78, 82
services, 6, 9, 16, 40, 41, 44, 53, 56, 58, 59, 63, 68, 69, 70
sexuality, 32
shape, 26, 33, 43
showing, 94
signals, 29
skewness, 86, 108
social change, xi, 77, 79
social contract, 74
social control, 6, 46
social deviance, 46, 50
social justice, vii, 4, 7, 9, 15, 16, 38, 39, 49, 80
social norms, 7
social policy, 5
social problems, 15, 16, 74, 77
social psychology, 23
social reality, 33
social responsibility, 74
social sciences, 117
social services, 58
social workers, 31, 46
socialization, 2, 46, 49
society, 2, 5, 6, 7, 11, 16, 38, 45, 47, 48, 49, 74, 75, 83
socioeconomic status, 79
sociology, 13, 22, 23, 51, 55
special education, 6, 38
spending, 54
stakeholders, 16, 40
standard deviation, 108

Index

133

state, 6, 9, 10, 11, 34, 42, 47, 48, 51, 55, 66, 73, 80

state custody, 9, 10

states, 2, 7, 8, 16, 24, 25, 29, 32, 47, 48, 52, 74

statistics, 86, 108

stimulation, 77

student populations, 92

style, 7, 44

summer program, 71

support services, 59

sustainability, 54

Swahili, 69

systemic change, 14

systems, 5, 6, 9, 10, 12, 14, 26, 31, 36, 41, 45, 47, 56, 81

Szasz, Thomas, 31

T

target, 39, 70, 81

teachers, 9, 16, 30, 39, 40, 41, 49, 59, 68, 78, 81, 92

teaching strategies, 9

techniques, 21, 26, 64, 67

technology, 82

teeth, 37

tensions, 20

test scores, 41, 79, 85, 86

testing, 9, 108

therapy, 56

thoughts, 16, 30, 53

time frame, 85

time periods, 107

top-down, 12

training, 68, 73

transformation, 82, 83

transformative change, 16, 83

treatment, 52, 77, 86, 92, 94, 96, 99, 107, 109, 110, 111, 112, 113, 114, 115, 116

tutoring, 59, 66, 70, 94

U

United States, 82

universe, 21, 22

universities, 12, 13, 15, 16, 40, 42, 73, 74, 77, 117

University Assisted Community Schools (UACS), 1, 4, 10, 14, 19, 20, 36, 37, 39, 40, 42, 54, 57, 58, 59, 61, 62, 63, 67, 68, 69, 70, 71, 73, 79, 80, 81, 82, 85, 86, 87, 88, 89, 90, 91, 92, 93, 94, 107, 109, 115

university education, 56

University of Central Florida, 42

University of Tennessee, 19, 20, 23, 37, 42, 54, 56, 57, 58, 60, 63, 66, 69, 70, 71, 80, 83, 121, 122, 123, 125

Urban Regime Theory, 15, 74

V

variables, 35, 86, 92

violence, 32, 45, 47, 48, 50, 52, 78

vouchers, 12, 13, 79, 80, 81, 117

vulnerable schools, 20, 81

W

wages, 40

walking, 17, 62

Washington, 3, 22, 120, 122

water, 28, 56, 77, 83

welfare, 9, 41

well-being, 15

Wisconsin, 8, 17, 55

workers, 41, 51, 81

workplace, 33, 51

Related Nova Publications

RACE AND ETHNICITY: INTERNATIONAL PERSPECTIVES, CHALLENGES AND ISSUES OF THE 21ST CENTURY

EDITOR: Sylvia Rivera

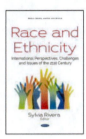

SERIES: Social Issues, Justice and Status

BOOK DESCRIPTION: *Race and Ethnicity: International Perspectives, Challenges and Issues of the 21st Century* first builds off the existing multicultural attachment literature to explore the concept of contextual and developmental adaptations of attachment bonds as it intersects with therapists' expectations for immigrant families living in the United States.

HARDCOVER ISBN: 978-1-53616-430-5
RETAIL PRICE: $230

INTERNATIONAL PERSPECTIVES ON SOCIAL THEORY

EDITOR: Jake M. Seery

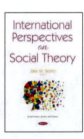

SERIES: Social Issues, Justice and Status

BOOK DESCRIPTION: International Perspectives on Social Theory opens with an identification of the characteristics that define contemporary social movements, including: a blurring and overlapping of taxonomical categories, an evolution towards a post-post-political stage, and a great variety and hybridization of organizational structures.

SOFTCOVER ISBN: 978-1-53615-991-2
RETAIL PRICE: $82

To see a complete list of Nova publications, please visit our website at www.novapublishers.com

Related Nova Publications

EMOTIONS, TEMPORALITIES AND WORKING-CLASS IDENTITIES IN THE 21ST CENTURY

EDITORS: Michalis Christodoulou and Manos Spyridakis

SERIES: Social Issues, Justice and Status

BOOK DESCRIPTION: This research aims to go beyond the theoretical state of the art in exploring class identities, class action and class formation (Bourdieu, Beck, Giddens, Foucault, E. P. Thomson, S. Hall) by adopting fresh and challenging theorizations that built upon the concept of time and emotions.

HARDCOVER ISBN: 978-1-53616-203-5
RETAIL PRICE: $195

PHOTOVOICE: PARTICIPATION AND EMPOWERMENT IN RESEARCH

EDITORS: Eva M. Moya, PhD and Silvia María Chávez-Baray, PhD

SERIES: Social Issues, Justice and Status

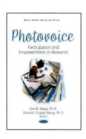

BOOK DESCRIPTION: "Photovoice: Participation and Empowerment in Research" describes Photovoice through the lenses of different communities and countries and discusses the methods and tools that make Photovoice appropriate for cross-cultural use.

HARDCOVER ISBN: 978-1-53616-201-1
RETAIL PRICE: $160

To see a complete list of Nova publications, please visit our website at www.novapublishers.com